cycling the
NORTHWEST

A solo trip from the West Coast to Green Bay,
through Bigfoot country

DAVID FREEZE

Published by:
Walnut Creek Farm Publishing
China Grove, N.C. 28023

Designed by Andy Mooney
Cover photos by Jon C. Lakey

ISBN 978-0-692-97229-8

Dedicated to Bradley Eagle,
1955-2017

One of my best friends.

FOREWORD

The Cascade Mountains were grueling. He could go miles and miles without seeing a single soul or building. And four miles from the finish line, his back tire went flat.

But if you ask David Freeze of China Grove, North Carolina, about his latest long-distance bicycle trip, his eyes will light up.

"It's almost as fun to talk about it as it is to do it," Freeze says.

And he's been "talking about it" with readers of the Salisbury Post for five summers now, setting out alone on his bicycle each year for another arduous journey. Throughout the trips, he sends nightly reports to the Salisbury Post to be published in the next day's paper.

His stories — part travel log, part observations about life — have developed quite a following.

David has been known for years as a runner; he's the long-time president of the local runners' club and even teaches running classes. Yet he has logged more than 15,000 miles on his bicycle over the past five summers.

Here's the rundown:

- **2013:** 4,164 miles from Astoria, Ore., to Myrtle Beach, S.C., in 54 days.
- **2014:** 2,850 miles, from Bar Harbor, Maine, to Key West, Fla., in 35 days.
- **2015:** 2,302 miles, from Mobile, Ala., to Owen Sound, Ontario, along the route of the Underground Railroad and beyond, in 35 days.
- **2016:** 2,778 miles, from Santa Monica, Calif., to Chicago on Route 66 and beyond, in 38 days.
- **2017:** 2,984 miles, from Anacortes, Wash., to Green Bay, Wisc., in 40 days.

The 2017 route was going to be a virtual straight shot, but David decided to add a roundabout 700-mile stretch to see the sights and check three more states off his list — South Dakota, Nebraska and Minnesota. David has now ridden his bike in 45 states, missing only Nevada, Utah, Vermont, Alaska and Hawaii. Eventually, he plans to cycle in every one of them.

Yes, even Hawaii.

If he hadn't detoured on the 2017 trip, he would have missed seeing the first rays of sunlight hitting Mount Rushmore early one morning. And he might never have tasted Twin Bings, a confection of cherry nougat, chocolate and peanuts that he declared "one of the best candies I have had."

Along the way, he pedaled up mountains so steep that he felt as though he might slide off the back of his bike.

Though it was summer, he saw snow as deep as three feet. He slogged through temperatures ranging from 37 degrees at the Washington Pass to nearly 100 degrees in drought-stricken Nebraska.

And then there was "the toughest storm I've ever been in in my life," with big winds, heavy rain and lightning. Why didn't he seek cover and get out of the rain? "There was nowhere to get out."

Food is important to someone expending so much energy, as you can imagine. Pineapple milkshakes are the go-to treat for David, who didn't eat much ice cream before he started these summer sojourns. Now he's addicted. "If it's not too cold, I can hardly ride by a Dairy Queen."

Another thing he can't resist is ignoring detour signs. "My thinking usually is to ride through and see what happens," he said.

Read on and you, too, will see what happens.

— Elizabeth Cook
Editor, Salisbury Post

ACKNOWLEDGMENTS

The credit for the fifth book in my series of cycling adventures has little to do with me, except that I got to make the journey across America's northwest. For me, that is the easy part and I reasonably know what to do in most situations. From that point on, the experts take over and turn out a first-class production.

The team again includes Salisbury Post editor Elizabeth Cook, author of the Foreword. She has also been the best cheerleader that I could imagine beginning with the first ride in 2013. Elizabeth has planned the annual celebratory return that has been so successful and appreciated. Creative director Andy Mooney has also played a huge part in the creation of the book but also the publishing of my daily reports from the road. Andy is actually mentioned in the book several times for going the extra mile to receive those reports. He provides the layout, design and graphics for the book and also serves as the final editor. Andy served along with copy editor Bobby Parker as my daily contacts. Jon Lakey returns as the expert photographer who has the ability to capture the essence of the ride each time and present it so well on both covers. All of these folks are truly creative and also wonderful friends.

New this year is lead editor Kathy Chaffin. She contributed a well-done critique of my writing and met a hard-to-reach deadline.

Special thanks this year go to contributors Fowler Physical Therapy and Dr. Delaine Fowler, Gentle Dental and Dr. Tanya Williams, Skinny Wheels Bike Shop and Eric Phillips, Vac and Dash and Peter Asciutto, Father and Son Produce and Linda and Tim Hoffner, Gear for Races and Luis Villareal, and Leonard Wood.

Things at the farm were managed quite well again by Sam Freeze and Ollie McKnight. Home issues were handled by my daughters, Ashley Baker and Amber Freeze.

Many others are named in the book for their communications and suggestions. Once again, I have been convinced that the support of the Salisbury Post and readers from near and far are one of the true measures of success of my ride and our literary efforts in general.

Truly, I know that I don't ride alone. My sincere thanks to God for another safe journey and to everyone who follows the cycling journeys for their support and interest.

INTRODUCTION

The riding continues, as well it should. Touring America has become my passion and maybe a little bit of an obsession too. Why? Because the real America that I love is still out there and there is plenty more to see. From little towns like Republic, Washington to Glidden, Wisconsin, the far away grass roots small towns are my favorites and you can ride along and get to know them just as I did.

A body is made to move and therefore at best when it stays in motion. On this tour of the Northwest segment of the United States, I visited Washington, North and South Dakota, Nebraska, Iowa, Minnesota and Wisconsin by bike for the first time and revisited Idaho and Montana. Yes, the bicycle took plenty of motion and you will read about the challenges incurred as I pedaled just short of 3,000 miles again from Anacortes, Washington, to Green Bay, Wisconsin. Nothing about the long journey was easy but rewarding and extraordinary became better words to describe the latest 40 days in the bike saddle.

That loaded Long Haul Surly bike causes conversation. When I stopped at a traffic light or next to my motel door, or even at the convenience stores that I love to visit, someone often approached wanting to know more. Those words exchanged quickly broke down any barriers of communication and within minutes, I had found a new friend and the resulting exchange usually became quite memorable. Other people came forward to offer memorable bits of the experience, as you will read about a farmer who parked on the other side of a busy highway and ran across to offer me a place to stay for the night. Or the Dutch lady who picked America's Lewis and Clark Trail for her first ever solo cycling adventure.

Now with five major unsupported trips complete and about 15,000 miles of travel, 45 states, all five Great Lakes and Canada are in my collected cycling bag. I have learned much about solo cycling but still the hunger for more knowledge and just plain fun continues. In this book, you will hear about the serious matters that occasionally include some danger and plenty of resulting comedic happenings. Humor is nearly as vital as prayer as the days go by. The physical challenges you will read about add to the excitement of the overall adventure. As always, there was plenty of sweat, some sore muscles especially in the beginning, long hours and lots of lasting memories.

So once again, it is time to settle back and join with me

as we pack up the bike to take you along to discover more of roadside America. I simply can't get enough of the experience made so much better by the connectivity with the readers. Here we go…

CHAPTER 1

How I got here

Nearly always, the saddest day of my bike adventures is the last day. It is then that I realize I am within 24 hours of being out of the saddle and away from the excitement and physical challenges of seeing the United States of America at an average speed of 11 miles per hour. Of course, that pace only applies to a good day, not the major climbing that often occurs at four mph or even slower. Still, well before another bike ride comes to an end, my thoughts are always leaping to the next.

Though my early bike rides got started in an odd way, they have now become an "every summer" adventure. Here's a brief recap of how it all got started. Back in 2011, I read about a small group that rode bikes on the rail trail along the Greenbrier River in West Virginia. The Charlotte Observer ran the story, and it sounded very interesting. My own history involved very little cycling but a whole lot of running, now nearing 82,000 miles over 39 years. The article recapped some of the challenges of riding the remote trail, even the possibility of encountering bears or other wild animals along the way. Early expectations included riding about 160 miles over three days during the late winter, and on a mountain bike instead of a road bike.

After a series of excuses to put off the Greenbrier ride, I finally loaded my bike into the back of my truck and started heading north on Interstate 77. A steady rain was falling, and the forecast was poor for my selected three-day sojourn into the wilderness, or as close to it as I had ever been on a bike. My drive ended later that morning in a parking lot at the trailhead. With excitement plus admittedly, a small dose of dread, I unloaded the bike from the back of my truck. It was an older model, very basic Trek which now seems to have vanished. I wish there was a good story I could tell you about how I lost it, but there isn't. It simply disappeared, and I can't remember when or how.

Back to the Greenbrier ride: For the first time in my life, I strapped onto the bike cargo rack some supplies in a couple of bags and a backpack over my shoulders and began to mount the bike. In the most embarrassing beginning imaginable, I quickly fell over the other side. From that first lesson, I realized that there was much that I had to learn about riding a loaded bike if only for a short trip. Although my remount was one of the quickest ever recorded and I don't think anybody even saw me fall, I was humbled from the start. Proper foot plant to brace the weight is a big step when mounting the bike. I will admit to doing the same thing, but usually from the mounting side on occasion later.

A quick recap of that first trip included a day of riding in the rain followed by a day in the gently falling snow and another of sunny but chilly weather. I loved the remote and historical environment along the naturally beautiful river. I was able to stay in the same town both nights — coming and going — and got a small taste of packing light and seeing very few people away from the town. I wondered if the "Beware of Bears" signs were really for me.

Physically, I was worn out at the end of the three days and sank deeply into the seat of my truck as I drove home. But more than anything, I was overwhelmed by the adventure of it all and knew before I even got a good start toward home that I wanted more. But, how could I get it?

I underwent knee surgery about a year later, just in time to give me another chance to explore the possibility of riding across the country on a bike route called the TransAmerica Trail. I had discussions with another successful endurance cyclist about what it would take and read some books about other similar journeys. With a mounting mix of excitement and apprehension, I decided to head to Oregon in early June of 2013, hoping to make the 4,000-mile journey in 60-65 days.

I do love a good adventure but as the days drew near, I wondered if I had taken on too much for my first long cycling journey. No one else was going with me and I planned to haul my own clothes, tools, supplies and everything else I needed for the duration of the trip. Still, I continued to read about all the successes and mistakes that other cyclists had made, although few of them went solo and unsupported.

The thought of having someone else riding along just didn't seem right due to the extreme physical challenges and my own rookie status. At least a few others said, "Why don't you ride with a tour group on this first one? Maybe get a better understanding of it all before you try a solo journey?" One thing was sure, I was going to either "make it or break it" on my own from the very beginning.

After riding a week on that first journey, I admitted to some struggles that included falling off again and getting slightly injured not once but twice. Both times, my hands and fingertips took a beating and the skin was torn by the pavement as I tried to catch myself. I vowed to not fall again on that trip. Traffic and persistent rain were issues in the early days as was the chilly weather. The up and down climbing with 40 pounds of supplies on the bike was harder than I expected.

But I will always remember the day that my plan seemed to be working after all these trials. Forgive me for not mentioning it before, but I am a freelance writer for our local newspaper, the Salisbury Post. Therefore, at the end of each day's cycling, I submit a recap of the happenings along the way. People, places, oddities, animals and sometimes just the boredom of the road and my resulting thoughts: it all comes together to make for a unique travelogue that surprisingly to me, many seem to find interesting.

Back to the day it all came together. Admittedly I struggled from the first day leaving Oregon and had some doubts
about the remainder of the trip. Late on that special day, I
rode into Sisters, Wyoming. An incredible coincidence happened when I stopped at a convenience store. Earlier, I had
to climb to a long mountain pass and stopped to get advice at a ranger station about which of two available routes
might be the best.

One female ranger took time to explain why she thought
I should take the longer but less steep road and I followed
her advice. From that ranger station to the convenience
store in Sisters was almost 50 miles, so imagine my surprise
to see the same ranger standing in line behind me at the
checkout. She was again very pleasant as we caught up on
my day.

I knew that it was getting close to my deadline to submit
my story to the newspaper, all the way across the country in
North Carolina. I called the nighttime editor and he told
me that we still had some time, so I began calling the local
motels and found them all to be very expensive and a few
of them already full. Another call to the local bike shop
confirmed that there were no affordable motels in town,
and my budget couldn't bear a high-priced motel just to
sleep and then leave with the approaching daylight the next
morning. Added to the mix was what looked to be a huge
thunderstorm coming from the west, just from behind the

beautiful Sisters Mountains. I figured I only had minutes to come up with a plan.

The bike shop owner told me that I might try some of the motels in Rawlins, Wyoming, just about 20 miles away. I had a couple of suggested ones and called to receive a very welcoming and inquisitive promise that an afford-able room was there if I could make it. So with the storm bearing down, I pushed the bike out into the traffic and started pedaling east, with the storm right behind me. The strong tailwind and reasonable terrain made for a fast ride of about 90 minutes to Rawlins just ahead of the storm. I called home and told a friend, "I can do this! What a great day!" From that day on, I have never doubted myself again, and there have been plenty of times I have made mistakes and certainly could have.

The cross-country ride ended successfully in Myrtle Beach, South Carolina. Right away, I was sad to see it end but I already had an idea for another route as a possibility for the next summer. The sense of adventure was so energiz-ing and fun that I never took a day off over 4,164 miles and 54 days. Some related health problems followed and with the help of some great medical folks, I kept on riding.

In the summer of 2014, I was back on my bike and rode from Bar Harbor, Maine, to Lubec, Maine, the most eastern point of the United States and then back by Bar Harbor on the way to the southernmost point in Key West, Florida. I had long ago discovered that while I loved seeing the sights along the way, the biggest reward to cycling travel was the people I met throughout the trip. About three days from the end of the ride, I was hit by a car and had the bike totaled from under me but still pushed on to finish the journey after purchasing another bike within an hour of the accident. More health problems followed.

Trip Number Three, during the summer of 2015, was possibly the most historic as I followed the trail of the Underground Railroad from Mobile, Alabama, to Owen Sound, Ontario, and addressed the crowd at the largest continuous emancipation celebration in the world. Along the way, I saw Niagara Falls, made my first sojourn into Canada and ended in Toronto from where it took more than a month to get my bike shipped back home.

A trip across the Mojave Desert during the summer of 2016 was part of my Route 66 adventure, from Santa Monica, California, to Chicago before adding on Indiana and Michigan. A high official temperature of 117 degrees, celebratory pies and the Blue Whale were highlights of yet another historic trip, this time along America's most famous highway.

As the summer of 2017 rolled around, I had a pretty good idea of where I wanted to go and some goals to meet along the way. With the previous rides, I had crossed 39 states and passed four Great Lakes and realized that a trip through the northwest or northern tier was the perfect succession to build those totals. In fact, I had considered this route the year before but gave it up in favor of the much more famous Route 66.

The same time frame was a good fit, with a planned departure of about mid-June and a finish in late July. Anacortes, Washington, seemed perfect for the starting point and I had reasons to point to Green Bay, Wisconsin, as the finish line. Originally, I wanted to follow most of the Adventure Cycling Northern Tier and stop when I got to Green Bay since the eastern states along that route were already in my bag. However, I did tell those closely associated with my plans that this one had the makings of a "figure it out as you go adventure," clearly the most fun of all for me.

Back in 2013, I was naive enough to believe that Adventure Cycling had considered all the options for traveling in a certain area, including interesting things to see. Just as I was about to make a turn following the map route in Kentucky, I saw a sign ahead of me about Lincoln's Birthplace National Park, just a half mile farther on the original road. Not following that map made me consider bigger options, not always the easiest, to go see more things. Multiple times over the years, I have used state driving maps and word of mouth from locals to find other interesting places. Heading into this trip, I planned to get road maps as I entered new states and set about adjusting the upcoming route as needed.

My equipment was ready once again. The tried and true Surly Long Haul Trucker is still the standard of endurance cyclists, tough enough to take a beating, stout enough to haul 40 pounds or more of material and easy enough to repair for most things that might go wrong. This Surly replaced the one I totaled in 2014 and was still like new after the Underground Railroad and Route 66 trips. The bike had been shipped ahead to the Skagit Cycle Center so it would be ready for pickup when I got to Anacortes.

Other important gear included my handlebar bag, originally purchased in Kansas after I saw other cyclists making good use of one. This waterproof bag generally carries those things that I need to grab quickly, such as my iPad, phone, wallet and other small supplies.

My panniers, though damaged in the 2014 wreck, were ready again. So were my leather gloves, cycling shorts, rain jacket, helmet and tool kit. All these items had made every trip so far. My tent was purchased in West Yellowstone in 2013 after the original proved to be quite leaky. I had the same half-body air mattress and small sleeping bag from the last three trips ready to go again.

As always, I spent much of the last week at home trying to accumulate all the information available about the states and towns I would pass through. Already, some of the locals weighed in with important information to be considered. I had a lot to absorb as time came to head west. But I was ready to go riding again.

CHAPTER 2

Washington — A mountain a day

A long day of travel to the west coast filled my agenda for June 11th. My daughter, Amber, dropped me off at the airport in Charlotte for a very early flight to Houston. I love to travel, and of course, that includes flying. Most travel days ahead of the bike rides have involved delays, and at least once, required multiple extra flights to get where I needed to be for the start of the 2013 cross country ride.

The bike and one pannier of my clothing, tools and miscellaneous other stuff were already in Anacortes, and I carried the other pannier and a backpack with me on the plane. We had packed very quickly on the day that we shipped the bike out of Skinny Wheels Bike Shop in Salisbury, and I realized too late that the very handy multi-tool was still at home. That was a mistake because the multi-tool was essential for the upcoming bike ride. The airlines don't allow carrying one on the plane so immediately I had a concern. But I decided if that was the only one, then I was headed for a good day.

My first flight was to Houston and then the connector took me to Seattle, where I was to ride a bus for about 2½ hours to Anacortes. I began to read the weather predictions for my first week of riding and already knew that the terrain was going to be challenging. During the travel day, I focused on looking ahead, considering options for how far I could bike on the first several days and what the climbing was going to be like. Small towns were the only options, which oftentimes are more of a crossroad than a real town. Cell phone coverage was likely to be very sporadic. All of this was a common thread with portions of the previous rides so there was little to worry about.

On a full plane from Houston to Seattle, the flight attendants were trying to make more space in the overhead bins and one of them dropped a bottle on my head just before we were set to leave. He apologized profusely, and I didn't think much about it until I looked in a mirror once we arrived in Seattle and saw the small knot. Most of the time on a plane, I don't do a whole lot of talking. But on this flight, I was seated beside Danielle, a young mother of two, who was terrified of flying. We talked throughout the whole time on the plane.

A pleasant surprise was that both flights to Houston and Seattle arrived early, something that I was assured would not happen. But it did, allowing me time to run through the airport and try to catch an earlier shuttle bus to Anacortes.

All of this worked out and arriving two hours ahead gave me a little time to look around after walking to my motel. The mistake of not shipping the multi-tool was offset after I found a few places to buy one on Monday before heading out of town.

By 1860, Anacortes had become a settlement on a harbor near Fidalgo Island. It was primarily used by whalers who accounted for much of the limited traffic in the area. Those whalers would stop at Anacortes for provisions. The town also served loggers and fishermen. Lumber camps sprang up everywhere and stripped the lowlands of wood, allowing farmers to move in after them. They found the land to be some of the most fertile in the west. Loggers moved up farther into the mountains because of the giant trees, which would eventually be named Douglas fir.

Having the extra daylight to look around town provided some quick highlights. Anacortes is a town with a population of about 16,000, believe it or not one of the biggest that I would see in the first four or five states. Cool temperatures greeted me as I arrived but that was expected. The Cap Sante Marina was one of the largest that I had seen in my travels, even along the Atlantic coast. A huge sternwheeler that had been used long ago to clear underwater stumps was moored alongside the marina and was very picturesque.

With my body still on east coast time, I woke up very early the next morning but tried to sleep a little longer to make up for the long travel day. I walked around as I waited for the bike shop to open and finally could stand it no more. I went to the bike shop and waited at the door hoping someone would come to work early and they did. I wanted to get the bike and head west.

I had to get a working red flashing safety light added to the back of the bike, and the cyclometer didn't seem to be working right either. The cyclometer provides speed, total mileage and a lot more data as I ride. It seemed to be OK as I left but the early trouble was a predictor of issues to come. Owner Gary Santiago had been so nice and helpful I didn't want to drag out a solution even more. He had other people waiting as he totaled my bill.

A comical situation happened next when I tried to get the ceremonial first photo as I dipped the rear tire in water to start the ride. On the way toward water options provided by Gary, I stopped at a boat shop and a hardware store to find a usable multi-tool. I was afraid to ride even one day without one and ended up buying one that was not only too expensive, but too heavy to add to my tool bag. I'll not forget to ship my lighter multi-tool from home the next time.

I tried to follow directions to find the water for the photo. I had been directed toward a boat ramp and finally found it but saw no people near the water. Making it even more difficult was the walk down a brushy path to access the water and the issue of needing to unhook my panniers from the bike to get a good photo. I kept working at it and still found no one so I decided to try to make a selfie. One other attempt to do the same thing several years before ended very poorly and so did this one. I made a few pictures holding my iPad high enough to see the back of the bike and the water and came away with a disappointing best photo.

With that, the bike ride east finally began. I was so ready but already a half day had passed. Town sizes decreased as I rode along State Road 20 east through Fredonia and then Burlington and Sedro Wooley, just before Lyman and Hamilton. My goal for the first day was to make about 60 miles, setting me up for a big climb the next day. The last larger town was Concrete, which got its name from many of the townspeople working to supply cement for the neighboring Ross and Diablo dams.

I passed through Rockport, a town with just one store that happened to be closed. The Totem Trail Motel, however, was open, and I spent the night there. By this time, the forests were thick, and the temperature had dropped to where it was almost cold. Every summer long distance ride has started in a logging area, and this one was no different. It was time for the climbing to begin.

Rainy Pass and then Washington Pass loomed large as I got up on a cold Tuesday morning. I had shipped heavier clothes ahead including seldom-used long pants and heavy mittens. I was at about 600 feet in elevation, but would climb to nearly 5,400 feet before the day was over. The last town was Marblemont and had an open store so I made good use of it.

Gold was discovered in the area in the late 1800s, but many of the miners became disillusioned and turned to logging as their livelihood or became shopkeepers, establishing Marblemont as a base for miners and trappers. Not much traffic was moving as I began a gradual climb up to Newhalen, the home of a spectacular dam and another closed store.

The hydroelectric plants were owned and operated by the city of Seattle. I began to notice lots more closed stores in the area as the real climbing began. Because of the uncertainty due to the all-day climb and being so early in the trip, I had no plans yet as to where I would spend the night.

Finally at about 6 p.m., I crossed over the snowy Washington Pass and headed down the much colder shady side of the mountain on a very fast ride to Winthrop, where I hoped to find a room. Washington Pass had views of Liberty Bell Peak, Early Winters Spires and Methow Valley, all amazing to me.

Due to the late hour back home in Salisbury, I called the night editor at the newspaper and talked with him about how soon I needed to send in my story. With my deadline fast approaching, I sat beside the road and typed out my daily update as the sun began to set. My iPad used Verizon, and I had just acquired service which allowed the call back to Salisbury and processing the update. I had never done this before. None of the mountainous areas in Washington had decent cell service.

The cold and wind had been significant on this day but

16

the wind proved to be a helpful tailwind. As much as three feet of snow had been on the ground in places, and temperatures had dipped into the mid-30s, rising into the 40s for most of the day. I had encountered only cloudy and cool weather since arriving in Washington. On this very long day, I had covered 90 miles as I headed into town in the near dark. My day was not quite over as I struggled to find a room.

Winthrop was an upscale Old West town with high-end priced rooms and wooden boardwalks. A tip from one of those upscale hotels sent me to a nice place called the Virginian. The office had already closed but I called the number on the door and was able to reach the owner. In another unusual twist to an already strange day, he told me that I would find two or three room keys in envelopes with the prices on them in the foyer outside the locked office door. Late arrivals could pick up one with the written price suitable to them and pay up in the morning. I picked up my envelope and found a very nice room at nearly 9 p.m., way too late after such a long day.

The only food available without another ride was at the high-priced convenience store next door, so I got what I needed for the evening and headed to my room. The stairs to my room were steep, yet another challenge for the day. Rolling the bike up the stairs with the bags still attached was too much, so I carried the bike up first and then went back for the bags. With the bike in my room, I enjoyed a quick but large meal and a shower before settling in a much-needed comfortable bed.

At this point on my ride, I had remained on S.R. 20 for the whole time since pedaling out of Anacortes. The owner met me in the office early the next morning and helped with some directions and told me about a major road repair on 20 that I would have to detour around. With the owner's suggestion, I decided to stop and ask the police in Twisp what the options were before I got to the actual detour.

It was a short ride from Winthrop to Twisp, where I found the police department was not yet open. I checked in at the local beauty shop and got the real scoop with information that the P.D. would be open in a few minutes. Just on time, the first to arrive was Police Chief Paul Budrow. He helped me with some information about the detour and pointed me toward a wonderful grocery store called Hank's.

There was a full service deli in the store, and I bought my first made-to-order egg and cheese biscuits of the trip. After that fine breakfast, I was ready to go check out the detour. Twisp, the birthplace of smoke jumping, had about 1,000 residents as compared to Winthrop, which had been much smaller with about 400. These towns would soon seem very large as I continued east.

I met Michael Miller from Twisp, and he told me about how he and his wife oftentimes put out a cooler of cold drinks for weary and thirsty cyclists. He had pulled over on the road to tell me that I couldn't get through the detour ahead. Just a little farther along, another resident was mow-ing her yard and walked out to tell me that I would soon be riding back down the road after being turned away. The road had been closed for months and no date had been set for re-opening. I thanked them both and just kept climbing.

With a little luck, I got around the detour and past all the construction in the area and headed over the mountain and into the next valley, one that looked like a different world. The huge fir trees were gone, and a high desert and views of majestic mountains became the norm. I saw lots of farm-ing, including apple and cherry production on hundreds of acres. Most of the fruit trees were under bird netting. Big wind turbines and even a helicopter were used for frost pro-tection. Numerous hay fields were either being irrigated or mowed all along the road.

I passed through Okanogan and Omak, the second of which was deemed a real town because it has a Walmart. I had heard that phrase before as I passed through sparsely settled areas. The rivers flowing in the area seemed so clean, and residents embraced them with parks and viewing areas.

Next up was Riverside as I continued to pedal along S.R. 20 on into Tonasket, a beautiful little town just at the base of tomorrow's next installment of the "Mountain a day" climb. Just before entering town, I was flagged down by a farmer who ran across the road to offer me a place to stay for the night. I politely declined because I had a place just ahead.

Tonasket was also the first town on the trip that I noticed

offering free camping, but I had called ahead to the Red Apple Inn and obtained a great price. The owner was quite entertaining as he told me about living in New York City and later showed me pictures of having run the New York City Marathon, something I had done four times.

Chris Zaferes also tried to adjust my attitude about baseball, the Civil War, Donald Trump and a few other things. He made a couple of calls for me to help line up motel options for the next day even though the weather was iffy and I had no idea where I would spend the night. His best line of the day might have been when I first called and told him I was on a bike headed for Wisconsin. "I have a room for you whether you bring the bike or not," he had told me.

Traveling in the western time zone puts me behind and shortens the available riding window each day, and it has been oftentimes stressful for me to submit my daily story on time. The amazing scenery and wonderful people made up for it but I still worried about adding stress for the newspaper folks back home. I nearly missed my deadline that night in Tonasket for the second time in a week.

The view outside my door facing tomorrow's uphill climb lingered on my mind, too. My legs were out of gas, and after 72 miles of biking, my quads were tender to the touch in a few places. More Washington mountains loomed just ahead. My mind was on both passes as I headed east out of the motel, after one quick stop to top off the bags early in the morning. The weather forecast called for cloudy skies with a chance of rain and cool temperatures.

It was a steady climb to top the Wauconda Pass after about six hours. Light rain, which fell off and on, wasn't much of a problem but multiple blind curves with some poor shoulders were. Sometimes the shoulders were perfect, smooth and wide enough to ride on, and other times they were missing entirely. There was lots of logging truck traffic and plenty of fast drivers on a road not made for either. Enough was going on to keep me on my toes.

Just before topping out on the Wauconda Pass, I heard voices behind me and was soon joined by three young cyclists. Brett Lehner and Sonali Rodriquez had just graduated from medical school and completed their residencies in preparation to practice medicine. They joined their friend, Joe Podurgiel, in spending the summer discovering America from Seattle to Connecticut. Brett said of their bike trip, "This will be our last summer off, probably for the rest of our lives. We want to make the most of it." Since they were traveling much of the same early route as I was, I expected to see them multiple times over the next 10 days.

The young cyclists from Connecticut and I rode into Republic, Washington, just as the rain intensified. The only other town, or closest thing to one during the morning, was Wauconda, Washington. The only store was closed but the post office was still open.

As the rain picked up, I had already spent half a day climbing Wauconda and decided to spend the afternoon eating, watching the rain and resting for the climb up the bigger and steeper Sherman Pass the next day. Sherman, at 5,575 feet, would be the highest mountain yet and having Republic as a jumping off point gave me a good chance to climb it and make some decent headway afterward. My motel had a covered balcony that faced down Main Street, also known as Clark Avenue, and I made the best of it. Tom, the owner at the Klondike, took special interest in my ride and gave me a super large room for a great price.

An exploratory walk downtown ended with an early afternoon breakfast at the Knotty Pine Café and some good conversation with historical content. Chelsea Jones and Anna Donner told me that I had just missed Prospector Days the last weekend and that gunfights in the streets were a big highlight. Republic had mined both gold and silver, ending in 1995 almost 100 years after it started. Lead ore was still mined according to supply and demand. Logging, however, was the current main industry.

The town was full of especially nice people. One thing I noticed right away was that every time I needed to cross the road, traffic coming both ways would stop while drivers waved me across. There wasn't a tremendous amount of traffic but the town of just about 1,100 people still seemed busy. Stores were open, and Main Street seemed to have plenty of purpose with very few closed stores.

Just before I got back to the room, I saw Joe and Brett again and they told me about going to a nearby fossil mine, where they had found a few rocks with fossils in them. "It was well worth the $10 it cost to look for them," Brett said. They headed for a Warm Showers host, someone who gives cyclists a free place to stay and evening meal.

I rode only 40 miles that day, frankly glad to be warm and comfortable as the chilly rain intensified. I planned to be ready for an early assault on Big Sherman the next day, and Idaho wasn't far away. But an easy afternoon in Republic, one of my favorite towns of all time, seemed perfect. While the rain played a part in keeping me there, a daylong rain was an unusual occurrence in a town that normally averages 12 inches of rain per year.

After all the great rest, I got up at 4 a.m. to take advantage of the first light to start climbing. Leaving Republic was easy and the terrain was reasonable, but about 10 miles beyond the pass, the grade steepened considerably. While the Wauconda Pass was a long and less steep climb, those last ten miles to Sherman rose sharply and major league views soon appeared everywhere. Signs about snow chains being needed and safe places to pull off to put them on were common. Logging trucks groaned as much as I did as we both struggled upward. The predicted rain did not materialize. Only small amounts of snow were near the top, much different than the three feet or so on Washington Pass earlier in the week.

Sherman Pass, at 5,575 feet, is Washington's highest pass that is kept open year-round. I was proud of the fact that the climb was completed by 10 a.m. It was still very cold at the top and the descent was likely to be colder. I put on all the clothes I had, including ski mittens, for the cold ride down the other side. The descent from Washington Pass had taught me to be better prepared for the cold this time and still have fingers pliable enough to work the brakes. Everything went much smoother as the riding was easy down to Kettle Falls, where all the logging trucks seemed to be going. It was on this portion of the ride that an unusual moment presented itself while I coasted down the mountain. With my cyclometer registering about 27 mph, a logging truck was slowly catching me as his engine brakes were screaming while they held the truck back. He seemed just off my left shoulder for a long time until he finally passed me and the ear-piercing noise moved on ahead.

In Kettle Falls, huge piles of logs were stacked right beside the wide Columbia River, much higher than I had seen before. Trucks kept coming from both directions dropping off more logs. Kettle Falls took about 50 miles of riding from Republic and another 10 on to Colville, where I would spend the night. Colville had at least one more huge pile of logs with the largest crane that I had seen. It moved along on high rails to pick up huge bunches of logs and quickly move them. I found it interesting that many of the log piles had water sprinklers running over them. I spent all of this day's ride on S.R. 20, my passage through the Cascades.

I was not aware before the ride that Washington had legalized marijuana sales. Bland looking sales outlets, usually away from other businesses, became quite common. Chris at the Red Apple Inn had told me that while the sales were legal, nobody wanted to have the outlets or pot fields next to their homes or businesses. Fences surrounded the growing fields, and I heard that some had mega lights along the edges of the fields.

After riding 60 miles for the day, I ended up at Benny's Colville Inn, a unique three-generation motel with a bike-riding owner. Andy and Teresa, his wife, were fun to talk to and gave me some insight on the road ahead. I looked forward to their early breakfast, too. I had one more night left in Washington and only about 1,500 feet of climbing ahead tomorrow.

One interesting story about Colville, Andy told me, was how raucous the town was at one time. It seems an Army lieutenant once shot a citizen in cold blood, just one example of the many tawdry things that went on. No one would testify against the officer, and he wasn't convicted of the crime. After that, town officials got together and decided to disband the local distillery and confiscate all the whiskey. The trouble soon cleared up in the formerly lawless town.

As mentioned before, I don't like climbing into a town and I like climbing out of one even less. Unfortunately, I often ended up climbing out of a town, which was usually a sign of a challenging day ahead. My favorite towns are gentle to enter and even gentler to leave. Not so with Colville.

First turn, first hill, simple as that. It was also cold until the sun came up. On my second hill about 10 miles out of town, I had my first flat of the ride. As always, I was thankful for it being the front tire as it was simpler and quicker to repair. I pushed the bike on up the hill, found a flat place to work on it next to a farm gate and changed the tube quickly, probably about a 15-20 minute process.

Shortly afterward, more rolling hills topped out at about 3,200 feet in elevation and I began the descent to the crossroads of Tiger, formerly a boomtown but now with only one store remaining. That store had been converted into a museum and had water and snacks inside. I was running a little low on both and the prices were excellent, so I stocked up while enjoying talking with the volunteer on duty. As I walked into the museum, I saw a cyclist ride up who had been sitting in the grass beside the road earlier as I descended into the town. Just as I came out, he rode away. I expected to see him over the next few days. I never did nor did I see the young doctors again.

At Tiger, I turned into a significant headwind for 46 miles on the way to Newport, my home for the night. I only passed a couple of small communities on the way, none with stores, so the water purchased at Tiger made the hard ride bearable. So did lingering views of the wide and beautiful Pend Oreille River. Newport got its name in 1890 because it was named as the landing site for the first steamboat to ply the river. The views on this day reminded me of the

Ohio River and at times of the Mighty Mississippi which I would see later.

The problem I had briefly experienced with my cyclometer, the bike computer, returned again. This time, it was worse, with mileage and miles per hour only sporadically working. The cyclometer totaled 83 miles for the day, the last one in Washington. Idaho would come next but I would remain in the Pacific Time Zone until the Montana border. That change would make my daily submissions less hurried, easier for me and also the editors back in Salisbury.

CHAPTER 3

Idaho and on into Montana — Bigfoot and the spoon

My night in Newport, Washington, went much differently than I had expected. Having called ahead, I had found a motel with a verbal guarantee of "Our WiFi is great, no one is complaining." Most nights, I ask that very question if I can call ahead. Only on a very few occasions have I been told that the WiFi was spotty, and honestly nearly every one of those times, the WiFi has been fine. Beware of the verbal guarantee!

I found my motel after a short ride from town and checked in. The first thing I had to do was get my update and photos submitted. I sent the photos first and noticed that they were just sitting in the outbox. I wasn't worried and knew that I could use my cell coverage if need be, so it was time to work on the daily update. I got it ready, in no real hurry even though darkness was quickly approaching. When I clicked the send button, I noticed that the photos still had not gone out. An attempt to send by cell coverage didn't work either.

A trip to McDonald's, a little over a mile away, provided the solution to getting my photos and update to transfer. As soon as I reached the restaurant parking lot, the outbox cleared. I called Andy back at the newspaper to make sure he had received everything. My update had not been received and neither was it still available on the iPad. I couldn't find it in my sent items and counted it lost in cyberspace. I asked Andy if I had time to write it again and he said, "Yes, if you hurry." As quickly as I possibly could, without maps or any reminders, I rewrote the story and sent it again. At nearly midnight North Carolina time, Andy received it and was able to get it in the next day's paper. This was by far the latest I had ever pushed the envelope. Thank you, Andy!

I expected to sleep a few minutes later the next morning after arriving back at the motel in the dark the previous evening, but I couldn't do it. Back on the bike, my first turn wasn't easy to figure out and I asked a local couple for directions. They told me the best way was along U.S. 2 and that I could follow it all the way to Sandpoint, Idaho. I was just a mile from the Idaho state line as I left Newport. I had two choices, following U.S. 2 or two smaller roads and a bike path on the other side of the Pend Orielle River. I took U.S. 2 for two reasons. It had been recommended by the locals and it would give me more time to bike along the river. Several towns dotted the route and this was not the case with the alternative. I passed the Idaho state line.

My pedaling route was upstream and the only real town

along the way was Priest River with about 2,000 residents. I passed through Laclede and Dover. A suburb of Sandpoint, Dover had 7,000 residents. Big mountains on both sides of the river made for a valley feel as I pedaled along the river.

In Sandpoint, I wanted to fix my malfunctioning cyclometer. Riding without a functioning cyclometer made it much more difficult to know when to expect turns and other points of interest. I had an idea of how to do it but I needed to buy two new batteries to make sure they were good. Several bike shops were listed in town, but none of them seemed to be open on Sunday afternoon. I stopped at a natural food store, and Rhyleigh told me where she thought I could find some batteries. She didn't know about the bike shops. Safeway, my favorite grocery store of all time, is where Rhyleigh sent me. I got the batteries and installed them, yet nothing changed. Nothing was registering on the screen. The basic graphics were there with no updates. I called the one bike shop that I thought might be open and found that it was not. The next one was at least two days away.

Once I got back on the bike, it seemed that all the traffic was headed the same way I was. Ahead was Lake Pend Oreille on S.R. 200 and I pedaled to the huge glacier-made lake around it, the traffic gradually thinning out. Winds across the water made it choppy, and only a few boats were out on the chilly and cloudy afternoon. Several marinas seemed devoid of much action.

The trains returned, and I enjoyed riding beside them. At regular intervals of about 30 minutes, another one came chugging by. Near the end of the ride, more wildlife was out, including deer and turkeys. I also met Mike and Wendy Fletcher from Prince George, British Columbia, when we stopped at the same time to read a historic marker about how a glacier formed the huge lake. They were riding a motorcycle and also headed to Clark Fork and eventually to Missoula, Montana. "I wasn't sure President Trump would let me in," Mike said, laughing. The cool temperatures kept me from wanting any ice cream but I knew that wouldn't be the case later. This was Father's Day, and I thought about my girls while singing a few hymns as part of my usual Sunday ritual.

I passed through the towns of Hope and East Hope, both small and quite scenic with historic structures that included a beautiful old church. The church was used for a wedding chapel, which made me nervous and forced me to leave the area in a hurry. I rode into Clark Fork next and found that my cellphone could pick up no signal on the edge of town. With only one available place of lodging, I wasn't sure what to think and figured to keep riding until I found the Clark Fork Lodge. After 60 fairly easy miles, I wanted to spend a nice Sunday afternoon exploring the little town. On my maps, no other towns were close enough to reach by the end of day. I pedaled through Main Street and saw a small grocery and a booming convenience store, spotting a sign for the lodge in the distance.

I rode on to the lodge hoping for the best. The person that I had emailed earlier for availability was not working, and a nice lady and her daughter seemed to be running the place. They were busy but noticed that I had ridden in, and both seemed interested in talking to me. I asked for an economical room and was quickly offered one at a high price. After telling her that I couldn't pay that much, she eventually halved the original quote and we struck a deal. The daughter showed me to the room, which included a small kitchen and just about everything else I needed, plus a view of the first uphill climb for the next day.

The lodge folks told me to go to the bar for food, or the grocery store if I wanted to make something myself. My cooking skills were so poor that I quickly smiled. After visiting the bar and failing to get anybody's attention, I stopped by the store and got a few things. The real place to be was the convenience store, easily the bedrock of the town. Choices for food, fishing supplies and much more kept a steady stream of folks coming through the doors.

Up and out early, I was on the road toward Montana at 5 a.m. The night had been especially restful and quiet, and I had a good feeling about today's ride. Each journey on the bike seems a little slow to get going and my legs take a while to get onboard, but there is always that certain day that I know it has all come together. This was that day on my current ride that I will always remember, and here's what happened. I know that bad things can still happen and there were huge physical challenges ahead, but this day was a big reason why I love these adventures so much.

Just eight miles into the day's ride was Montana, a state that I already loved. Still without a working cyclometer, I followed the mileposts to keep my bearings. Riding on S.R. 200 and along the picturesque Cabinet River, there were some good ups and downs. With little traffic, and almost none on my side of the road, this portion of the morning was extremely scenic and peaceful. There were no towns listed for the day until I reached the night's lodging later in Libby, Montana.

The biggest surprise of the day was a small country store called the Big Sky Pantry. I was hungry and stopped in to at least get something different to eat and take a break from the bike. I met Beth Morkert, who runs the store with a smile and a twinkle in her eye. She told me the store had been open for almost 20 years and includes all kinds of freshly baked goods and a deli. Beth told me that a cyclist once bought a whole pie and ate it all out front before leaving. I just bought a cinnamon roll, a large oatmeal cookie and two fudge brownies. It was a dumb move on my part not to buy two or three times that much.

Beth also told me what to expect on the road ahead. She said it wasn't especially hilly and that there were only a couple of challenging places. Usually when I get those adjectives about an upcoming ride, I move right away into some serious climbing. It turned out that Beth was exactly right as I turned onto S.R. 56 and followed it for 35 miles. This portion of the ride was the most scenic of the trip so far. Mountains in the distance and the Bull River up close make for beautiful scenery. The hills were so manageable that my legs felt great, probably because I kept stopping to eat some of Beth's pastries. Signs called for bighorn sheep but I never did see any. Another sign told me that I had just missed the Yaak Sasquatch Festival. Sounds like a perfect place for that event.

I missed out on the sheep but had an unusual encounter with a big deer. He came out of the woods as I rode by. Usually they run back into the woods, but this one did the opposite. He ran out to the road about 50 yards behind me. I stopped, and he did, too. Just as I started to take pictures, the deer began trotting slowly toward me. When he got to within 50 feet of my bike, a truck came around the corner and scared him away. Do you think he wanted one of the brownies?

Beth and the deer were just the beginning of a great day. Huge mountains formed a fantastic backdrop as I passed Bull Lake, which must feed into the river of the same name. I noticed a thump-thump as I continued to pedal east. Usually that dreaded noise meant something was in the tire and a flat was coming. This time, I stopped and picked up the front of the bike and spun the front tire. The "thump" was only a piece of asphalt that had stuck to the tire. I just peeled it off and was immediately on my way.

Part of the multitude of things that help pass my time on the bike have been personal challenges of various types, such as a goal of time to climb a mountain or reach a certain intersection. I knew that the intersection of U.S. 2 was coming up, and I said to myself, "It's going to be hard but I want to try to make it in 22 minutes." Right away, a segment of new asphalt and some downhill appeared. I made the last four miles to U.S. 2 in 17 minutes and used part of the time saved to visit a roadside bathroom.

Feeling especially strong, I turned on U.S. 2 toward Libby. On the way into town, I stopped to see Kootenai Falls where a rushing Kootenai River does its own smaller version of Niagara Falls and added more to an already picturesque day.

Just after the falls, I started to think about a continuing issue that concerned me. I had to change a tube in a flat tire the other day as I left Colville and broke one of the little plastic tools that are used to separate the tire and the rim. The same tool is used to reseat the tire and rim, and at present, I only had one, not enough to do the job because it takes at least two. Right after Colville, I saw a metal spoon lying beside the road and didn't think much of it. Too late, I realized that the handle of that spoon would do the work of the broken tool. Thinking that God had placed the spoon there for me, I should have picked it up. Since I knew how forgiving God is, I thought, "Well, if He did it once, I bet

He will do it again." Not five minutes later, I found a metal fork beside the road. I realized that the fork would do the same job. God sent me the message to open my mind. It didn't have to be a spoon at all!

Unsure of where to stay in Libby, I wanted to put the proper end to a great day. I stopped at a campground to check it out, and Sharon Falls and Barb Woolsey worked hard to get me to stay. They offered incentives that were hard to resist but I knew that plenty of motels were in town. Usually, that meant I could find an economical deal. After calling several motels, I began to consider the campground again until I stopped in at the Country Inn. Right away, I pitched my ride as a reason for a good deal and noticed that the motel had freshly-baked cookies and free water. I got a real deal and checked in before I felt entitled to the free cookies.

An all-day breakfast restaurant was next door, and that's where I had my evening meal. I had hoped to turn in a little early, but the bright daylight after 9 p.m. kept me up. It was still bright enough to easily catch a baseball at 10 p.m. This culminated my best day yet on the northwest journey.

Libby had been the site of the first fur trading business in the northwest, aptly named the Northwest Trading Company. Another fact noted that Libby had vermiculite discovered nearby and at one time supplied 80% of the world's needs. W.R. Grace and Company, a huge horticultural company, bought the rights but later found that the Libby vermiculite contained asbestos. Sadly, a significant number of local workers died from exposure.

The tradeoff for that late light was a darker morning, and I couldn't hit the road until 6 a.m. Just as I started to leave town, I saw a wooden cutout of a Bigfoot carrying a bag of money away from a Libby bank. This was definitely Bigfoot country, and I realized that Bigfoot families have to bank somewhere and mostly likely need necessities just like the rest of us.

All my maps and other information showed a series of challenging hills for this Tuesday. I pedaled away from Libby along S.R. 37 for about 15 peaceful and scenic miles. All of this changed when I approached the Libby Dam. S.R. 37 had been rerouted way up above the river during the construction of the dam. The road was aggravating in that the pavement wasn't the best, and the water views were blocked by thick trees. An earlier option of taking the road that traveled the other side of the river seemed to have been a better choice but I had no way of knowing for sure.

Trees and rolling hills continued until about 45 miles into the trip where I was blessed with good views of Lake Koocanusa, where the river water was held back by the dam. As I climbed one of the more scenic hills with its own rock formations, I saw Theresa Lawrence starting to climb a huge rock wall by hand beside the road. Rob Larsen was belaying her from the ground. While watching and helping Theresa, Rob told me that the state had many rock-climbing venues along S.R. 37. He said they came from Sparwood, British Columbia, often to enjoy them. I watched Theresa climb and found it fascinating.

The weather had changed several times during the morning. The still and mild weather in Libby became drizzly and chilly by late morning. By the time I met Rob and Theresa, the sun had come out and the wind was really blowing as the temperature quickly rose into the mid-80s.

I kept riding and finally ended the day at about 4 p.m. in Eureka after 70 miles and not much to show for it. I saw a couple of deer, a possible eagle and a huge new bridge that had an eerie sound coming from it. All the cables and connectors must have made the noises as the strong wind blew through them.

Another day without towns ended when I pedaled into Eureka and found the Silverado Motel, one with great WiFi. My plan was to find plenty of food and then work on the bike cyclometer. I had finally been able to reach the Sigma technical support guy late in the day, and he told me several things to try. He also said I could email him with any questions and that he would answer. I had tried to call for two days and when I got him, our connection was so poor that I wanted to get all the information I could. I was only about 10 miles from the Canadian border and in sparsely settled land.

Much of my planning on Tuesday evening had to do with the upcoming Glacier National Park. There was much uncertainty about what I could do on the bike and where I could actually ride. The famous "Going to the Sun" road was closed still from the heavy snows of winter and not expected to open by the time I passed through. Bikes were only allowed on the road before 11 a.m. and after 4 p.m., making me concerned about what I could do during that five-hour period even if it did open. I was also looking ahead to gather information on the best way to enter Canada after the park. There are not many roads to choose from in this area and I wanted to make good choices.

I did get a chance to work on the bike cyclometer that evening. There was plenty of room to take the parts of the small sensors and examine them. I made sure to put the batteries in correctly and extend the tiny little connection the way the technical guy told me and to close the cover exactly the way he said. After several tries, I was amazed to find it working and very excited that I could just watch the mile markers as I rode by and not have to monitor them anymore. Not sure exactly which thing worked, I hoped that the cyclometer would work during the next day's ride. The lighting was dim in the room, and it was nice to have plenty of late afternoon sun to help illuminate the tiny parts as I worked.

The longest days of the year made that late day sun pretty remarkable. It just simply was not dark yet when I needed to go to bed. People seemed to be out and about late as I watched two thunderstorms way off in the distance in this great example of the "Big Sky" country. One lady told me about once seeing four different weather conditions out the windows from each corner of her house.

Eureka was once known as the "Christmas Tree Capital of the World." Actor John McIntyre was raised there and also buried along with his wife, actress Kathleen Nolan. With about 1,000 residents, it looked a lot bigger than I expected from the dot on the map. Canadian and BBC channels were predominant on TV.

I left on Wednesday morning by riding through Eureka on S.R. 93 and experienced a huge climb leaving town. There were several other major climbs but plenty of moderate stretches as well. Now that I could track my own mileage again, my 64 miles on this Wednesday included plenty of deer in the morning and also plenty of road shoulder to ride on.

The first town was Fortine but it was off route and needed a side trip to see it. I decided not to go there. Next came Stryker and Olney, both very small and the latter with a population of 26. My first real town was Whitefish, home of Glacier Cycle where I planned to get some supplies and information. Mark Ambre, who worked in the local bike store, told me all about how to get over or around Glacier National Park. The road over the top was still closed but Mark said he had heard that it could open any day. I was right about the restrictions but Mark thought he knew how I could get through. He suggested that I ride as far as I could and then drag my bike across the snow at the top. Mark was fun to talk to but I decided that my only real option was to take U.S. 2 around the edge of the park, thus missing the "Going to the Sun" road this time. Mark sold me the supplies that I needed, and we made a few photos. His bike store didn't sell Montana maps.

From that point, I decided to leave the Adventure Cycling route for the rest of the day. Before I left town, I stopped at a book store and asked about a Montana map. They didn't have one either but one of the clerks gave me some insight on an upcoming intersection that she thought was particularly dangerous for bicycles. I took note and headed south of Whitefish. I wanted to get to at least Columbia Falls that afternoon. Somewhere in that area would be my jumping-off point for the ride through Glacier National Park.

Already in the touristy section that surrounds the park, I knew that the search for an affordable place to stay was going to be a challenge. I started calling and checking my phone as I finally did have good reception. One of my first calls was to the Glacier Inn Motel, and the owner gave me a price that seemed high. But after calling several more, I decided to go ahead and just pay the price as a "one and done" to keep moving.

As I got closer, I called to confirm that I did want the room and found the motel right on my way toward the park. Closer to the entrance would have been better but not required since I could get up early and make up the distance with hopefully less traffic. What I found was almost a perfect setting in an older but very attractive motel. Carla Rummage and her husband had talked about my ride and decided to give me a special price, way more reasonable than anybody else that I called.

The room was huge and faced a beautiful view of the park and some of its eastern mountains. I was still about 20 miles from the park entrance but the mountains made it look much closer. With the first distant views of the park, I could see just a little bit of the ice and snow. The many glaciers that remain in the park today are what some geologists called "shriveled vestiges" of the magnificent ice fields once there. Geologists say that barring a major change in climate, it will take about 1,000 more years for all the remaining glaciers to disappear. I was excited about getting a closer look.

Very happy with my choice for the night, I walked back to a bustling sub shop that had homemade cookies. I bought plenty for an evening meal and walked back to the room. For the first time on this trip, I had decided to go for a walk every evening that I possibly could. My legs needed it and I just simply felt better to work the kinks out of my legs after pedaling all day. I had in mind the blood clots from previous years too and hoped that the walking might help with that. Possibly it had been a mistake to go directly from the bike to the chair at the end of the day. I hoped to avoid those blood clots as a result of this ride.

Carla introduced me to her grandchildren when I stopped

by the office to ask about a Montana map. I was determined to find one soon. Carla showed me a map but couldn't let me have it because she didn't have another. She did show me the roads that I would use the next morning and told me that at least one stretch could prove to be quite dangerous because of the almost non-existent shoulder. In fact, I later read that the Adventure Cycling route chose to avoid this segment because it was rated as narrow and dangerous. An early departure would mean less traffic on the road. We took photos of each other, and I headed back to the room for what I hoped was a restful evening.

A couple of interesting things happened late, one good and one bad. I had been told by Carla that there was a sort of visitor's center right across the street. She said they kept lots of their information in racks outside, and she was almost sure that I could find a Montana map there. At just before dark, I walked over to see what was available. There were a lot of good pamphlets and coupons, but not a Montana map in sight. What I did find were two huge brownie-like cakes wrapped individually. I mean huge for brownies, not huge for cakes. Originally thinking that they were there for anybody, I took one and brought it back to the room. Right away, I began to worry that the dessert treat was meant for someone else. First thing the next morning, I took it back. That was considered the good thing.

The bad thing was a loudmouth guy who showed up late that afternoon, apparently upset that he had been recently fired from a place that another man from a couple doors down knew a lot about. They sat outside and moaned and groaned while using plenty of foul language. This was the perfect room to leave the windows open on a comfortable night but I couldn't stand to listen to the exchange a minute longer. I actually sat outside for a few minutes and they went in the room, but as soon as I left, they came out and continued the tirade.

I spent much of the evening reading about Glacier National Park. One of the most interesting legends concerned the road that I would not get to use. From the park east, much of the land has been Blackfeet Indian territory for centuries. It seems that at one time, the Blackfeet had been visited by much adversity. They were no longer good at war, were immersed in famine and their skills were diminished. The Great Spirit, seeing this, sent among them a warrior chief who knew all things. The Blackfeet regained their dominance over other tribes and all was well. The warrior chief left as quickly as he had come, climbing up high in the mountains amid thunder and lightning. After the storm cleared, the sun came out and the Blackfeet saw that the snow formed a profile of the great chief as he was going to the sun.

At some point, my neighbors shut up and the rest of the night passed peacefully enough. I looked forward to a great day tomorrow.

CHAPTER 4

Glacier National Park and the rest of Montana

Nothing about my current ride had involved so much discussion as Glacier National Park and how to get there, move through it and exit in the best way possible. The "Going to the Sun Road" and Logan Pass were primary goals when I began reading about the northwest area attractions. Thursday, June 22, was my day to see the park.

I departed at 5:45 a.m. amidst light traffic and a very cool temperature of 44 degrees. I thought I had a plan but what I really had was a great deal of uncertainty and an ongoing sense of adventure. I was back on U.S. 2, a favorite road that would nearly let me down on this day. The first town was Hungry Horse, an interesting place that had listed several motels, only one of which I found affordable. I had gotten no answer when I called the previous day and was interested to see if I could find it while riding through.

As it turned out, I did see it and the small motel parking lot looked full, which may have been the reason that no one answered when I called. The two higher-priced motels didn't look anywhere near capacity. Since that was yesterday's news and I had bigger things on tap for today, I smiled and kept riding.

On display in Hungry Horse was a huge wrecking ball, nearly as tall as me. It was suspended somehow between two tractors and used for land clearing and immortalized for everyone to see on the way to Glacier Park.

I found a very good bike path in the same area and rode along it for a while until it ended and I, of course, got back on the road. The time was just after 7 a.m. when a motorist pulled over to tell me that the police would ticket me for riding on the road. This was not a busy road at that time of morning so I thought his comment was amusing but didn't say so. I just kept riding and in fact, stayed on U.S. 2 for the rest of the day and a large portion of the rest of my trip.

I arrived at West Glacier, the official entrance to the park, at about 8 a.m. A bunch of shops not yet open, an Amtrak station, a hotel and convenience store/restaurant were all located near the entrance. Hungry and in no special hurry, I ordered two pricey egg and cheese sandwiches with plans to eat them while I watched the Empire Builder passenger train come and go. After eating the biscuits and with still no sign of the train, I decided to ride on. The eager passengers, most from somewhere in the park, kept looking down the tracks toward the train's expected arrival.

U.S. 2, which would later become more like a wonderful

friend, actually scared me quite a bit that morning. For the first 10 miles or so, the edge of the road was crumbling, and the road itself was not wide enough and ran through a series of blind curves. Add to the mix ever-increasing traffic that included plenty of RVs and a few large trucks. At times, riding on this road felt very unsafe. On one particular blind curve, I walked the bike, struggling to balance it and myself on the narrow lip of a ditch. All of this reminded me of my extreme dislike of the traffic issues around Yellowstone Park when I rode through in 2013. Every long distance cyclist I met had so looked forward to riding in the fabled park but was concerned about safety, with significant traffic and road issues overshadowing the expected joy.

The riding was slow as I started to climb U.S. 2 but the scenery was beautiful as I rode along the Middle Flathead River, many of the backdrop mountains still covered in snow. Montana has the bluest sky and some of the greenest water I have ever seen, both adding to the beauty. Just at the moment when I had stopped to take a few photos, a group of raft riders enjoying the rapids all waved in unison to me. Of course, I waved back before riding up another long hill toward another spectacular river overlook.

It was on this uphill ride that I spotted a cyclist coming toward me. Jack Day pulled over and I walked my bike across the road. Often when long distance cyclists see each other on the road, we enjoy meeting and sharing information about our trips. Jack had a full set of bags mounted on his bike and appeared to be an experienced long-distance cyclist. He told me that he had started in Hilton Head, S.C., and planned to ride to San Francisco. Jack was 74 and had already cycled in every state except Vermont, also among the five in which I had not yet cycled by the completion of my current ride.

The most unusual thing about Jack was that his bike had an electric assist motor mounted on the frame. When I commented on it, he said, "Just wait until you are 74, you'll see. If dogs get after me, I just pull away from them." Jack gave me a pack of peanut butter crackers, vowed to stay in touch and we wished each other "Safe travels!"

Close to the top of the hill and high over the river, I noticed two people with cameras walking along the edge of the road. They were photographing four mountain goats walking just below road level and about to go under the highway. I got there in time to also grab a few photos of the goats, on their way back from a natural salt lick.

Continuing my ride around Glacier Park on U.S. 2, I spent the long afternoon meeting hundreds of vintage cars coming toward me. Most were wonderfully restored and the motors sounded strong as they passed me. The drivers and passengers waved, and I waved back. There must have been one heck of a car show somewhere nearby that weekend.

The final major climb of this journey was now under way as I pushed on toward Marias Pass. Before the last ascent, I spotted several cars pulled over on the right side of the road, usually a sign that something good was just ahead. This time I could see a major waterfall, one of the best of this trip, just on the other side of a few trees. The best view was from the bottom of the waterfall and I climbed down to get that shot. Others did the same, but the interlude was probably better for me than all the car riders.

The weather started getting colder and a headwind developed as my push to the pass continued. Marias Pass, also part of the Continental Divide, was dominated by a snowy mountain panorama to the north. Those sheer mountains were the pictorial highlight of the day, just before what I anticipated to be a long gradual and enjoyable downhill off the pass.

What I found was that U.S. 2 took on a different perspective on the downhill side. A huge rush into the park from the east intensified as the afternoon progressed, often with long lines of traffic speeding toward me. The road itself narrowed as did the shoulder, leaving me less room to ride although by this time much less traffic was exiting the park area. Because of this, those long lines of cars going west took advantage of open spaces to do plenty of passing. No passing zones were clearly marked but even those were ignored while the sight of a speeding car barreling toward me in my lane was another spooky event. At least twice, the cars were coming so close that I quickly got off the road. Did it matter that much to pass a couple of cars at this very moment? Another reminder of the great traffic rush around

Yellowstone and the desire for breakneck speed while in the presence of such natural beauty.

The cold, chilly and often harrowing ride wasn't quite as downhill as I expected. The eastern facing slope still had plenty of short inclines, often blind ones that limited lines of sight for approaching traffic. Just over 74 miles of rugged riding for the day finally came to an end at East Glacier, at least the main part of town. East Glacier was still part of the Blackfeet Nation, and a plentiful Indian presence was easy to see in the town. I had called the night before and made a tentative reservation at Jacobson's Cabins, the best rate I could find largely because of lodging demand for the next day's half marathon. The first several places I called were already full of runners and pointed me toward Jacobson's, making me wonder if there was anything wrong there.

During the day, I had another spoon encounter. I just happened to spot a similar style spoon alongside the ride and this time, I stopped to pick it up. I now had a fork and a spoon, both of which I would continue to carry as good luck charms considering the significance of the offering of the first spoon, the acceptance of the well-placed fork and now it's almost matching spoon. Along with Patsy McBride's angel, I expect the spoon and the fork will ride with me as I continue traveling by bicycle.

When I entered the town, I could not recognize any of the motel names that I had called and asked where to find Jacobson's. I was told that a different portion of the town was less than a mile away and that most of the accommodations were located there. Just at that time, I saw another cyclist riding into town from the east. I caught up to him, and we talked briefly. He was from Ohio and had no maps and no real itinerary. Perhaps no money either as he asked if I knew of a place where he could camp for free and if there was a library for WiFi. Local resident Mike Anderson stopped by to help us both out with good information, just before we headed off in opposite directions.

I rode toward Jacobson's, finding a different kind of town, this one trendy with an international feel to it, while setting at the base of yet another panoramic backdrop of Glacier National Park and the Cascades. Any concern I had about the cabin was quickly dispelled as I rode onto the property. Large cabins with their own parking spaces were neatly arranged with views of the mountains. I went to the A-framed office and signed in, where the owner assigned me to Cabin #4, easily remembered because I still have the key after forgetting to leave it when I rode away. But Cabin #4 was amazingly large and modern, well-furnished and clean, all things that I usually look for at a low-ball price. Not so low ball this time!

Since I was late and still in the western time zone, I had to get my daily story in to the Post. The owner had told me that his WiFi and most of the others in the area were spotty. All day, I was concerned about this because cellphone connectivity was also spotty at best. The owner was ready for me and gave me a little black box smaller than most cellphones to use for WiFi, a method with which I was unfamiliar. Wireless and battery powered, I took the little box back to my room and immediately logged in and found it worked perfectly.

With my story and updates submitted, I headed out to return the box and explore the little tourist village. Two restaurants were quick choices, so I headed into the busier one. I took a menu and ordered a veggie burger to go from a waitress who didn't seem to understand English. In fact, I noticed that many other languages were being used around me. A nearby hostel probably had something to do with this, but I wondered what brought all of the foreigners of student age to East Glacier. It also made me wonder what I would get in or on my veggie burger. Another waitress came over to tell me to expect at least a 30-minute wait on my order. Still wanting to explore the rest of the village, I told her that I would come back in 30 minutes.

A bakery was located next door, and I felt the pull of some large-size brownies and cookies. A good brownie can solve just about any issue and with no pressing concerns, I planned to eat these for enjoyment. The reasonable prices on water reminded me to get some more for my bags. I found the local-proclaimed largest purple spoon in the world nearby and wondered if I could tie this huge utensil into my own spoon saga somehow. A hostel and a very nice lodge added to the trendy feeling of this little village, and I was constantly drawn to the view of the mountains.

Back to the Whistle Stop Restaurant for my veggie burger, I was handed a very light styrofoam box. I asked whether the fries were in there and it's a good thing I did. The English-speaking waitress went back and added them, but I found later that I should have checked to see what was on the burger itself. Apparently, if you don't order condiments separately, you end up with only a burger and a bun. However, I didn't discover this until I was back in my room.

At this point, I had no idea how to proceed toward Canada the next day. My track out of Glacier National Park was supposed to be from the main road, the "Going to the Sun" road. I still didn't have a good Montana map and asked about one at the motel office. The owner's wife said, "They are so hard to find that we hardly ever have them. Come back in a few minutes, and talk to my husband. He will know what to do." I went back to the room and pulled out my Montana information and checked out the apparent options while eating. It looked to me that Adventure Cycling was directing me to more sparse country for one day in Canada and then a return trip to join up with U.S. 2 to continue east. I decided to ask the owner and Leonard Wood back home whether I would miss anything by skipping Canada this time and using the extra day to visit Nebraska later. Nebraska was still on my list to cycle into on this trip, especially since I was going to be so close.

I went back to see the owner and his insight was wonderful, almost assuring that my plan had just been nailed down. Leonard's text later confirmed that the time would be better used by taking the Nebraska route. While not necessarily easier, I had a clear plan to proceed in the morning.

The cabin was so nice that I hated to spend so little time enjoying it. I had read on the reviews that the water sometimes comes in rushes of hot or cold when taking a shower and that the TV channels were very poor. The shower did make me jump a couple of times and the TV had just a few good channels, but really none of that mattered. I loved the room and the fact that it had a good heater. By dark, it was already getting cold and a low of 37 degrees made the heat come in handy.

I dressed for cooler temperatures the next morning and headed out by myself on a lonely U.S. 2, excited to be off the mountains for the first time since Washington. Right away, hay fields and pastures with plenty of cows lined the road. One big surprise was a huge herd of buffalo that I enjoyed seeing. They were next to the road, possibly enjoying traffic and more so, a marshy area that had some standing water. Many of the buffalo just stood still in the water even with the cold morning. I stopped to take photos along with others doing the same. Even more photogenic was the best panorama yet of the mountains as I rode away to the east. The sheer size of the range was apparent as the western sky, from as far as I could see north to south, was filled with snow-patched mountains. This was another one of the views that made me forget the last one and be amazed yet again. I kept riding east and didn't lose sight of the Cascades until about 60 miles later.

The first town of the morning was Browning, listed as the tribal center of a segment of the Blackfeet Nation. What I found to be the highlight of the town was my introduction to a chain called Taco John's, home of fantastic egg, cheese and potato burritos. I have since started ordering the same thing from Taco Bell back home. Browning is also the home of the most broken glass I have ever seen along the roadways. I am not sure why so much of it was there but I had to focus just ahead of the bike tires to watch for the biggest chunks. As I rode east, an early headwind started to kick up and added to the chill in the air. I kept my mittens on.

A tandem bike rode up beside me and the driver spoke, so we pulled over to talk as I was introduced to Dave and Joanne Ryan of Seattle. The Ryans had taken the summer off to ride across the country in honor of their 45th anniversary. "Our kids aren't too sure about us doing this, and they are keeping close track of us," Joanne said, laughing. We talked about mutual issues of concern, including the glass on the road, bike shoulders and the crazed drivers around Glacier Park that made the poor roads and shoulders so dangerous. Dave had acquired a three-foot stick with a flag on it and attached it to the back of his bike to keep drivers the required distance away from him as they pass. "Don't you get tired of pulling your elbows in?" he asked me.

We talked about planned overnight stops for the next few days and how we hoped to see each other again. As they rode away, their four legs increased the distance until they went over a hill and out of sight. Dave's three-foot stick and flag was not a hit with drivers who chose to honk at him as he continued to "take the lane" with his bike and flag. I never saw the Ryans again but did hear about them much later in the trip at an overnight stop.

The next town was Cut Bank, billed as the junction between the Rockies and the plains. I was very ready for some of those plains especially if they turned out to be as flat as I had perceived. Cut Bank was still part of the Blackfeet Nation and home of the steepest incline into a town on the whole trip as I pedaled almost straight up from Cut Bank Creek to the main town. A fantastic convenience store gave me plenty of choices to load in my bags for the rest of the day.

I pushed on for a total of 74 miles into Shelby, home of a rich cowtown history and a major switching station for the railroad. Herds of cattle were brought to Shelby and then driven to North Dakota. Cowboys used to say that the cattle drive could be done without cutting a fence, reminding me that great plains used to be just one giant common pastureland.

I learned a good lesson while in Shelby. There were several motels in town, including a listing for the Totem Motel. Jim, the owner, gave me a super price over the phone, but his directions for getting to the motel seemed confusing. When I finally found it, I was across the bridge from the town in a residential area. The motel looked rough from outside, but as I have said often, "I am only going to be here to sleep and will be gone very early." I actually hesitated about going into the office, but Jim was waiting for me. Before I paid, I asked to see the room, hoping secretly that it would be a dump and I could just leave. The room turned out to be just fine but I was still a little worried about the area. Jim seemed to anticipate my questions and had answers for everything. I spent the night, enjoying one of my most restful evenings ever and had all the amenities but ice. A trip back across the bridge before dark took care of food and ice and once again, I had stumbled into the right place. Don't decide what is inside the package before you unwrap it!

Throughout this day, I became even more sure that the choice to bypass Canada and go way off route to South Dakota and Nebraska soon was the right one. There was a lot of uncertainty ahead and even though I was still on the Adventure Cycling maps, the next day looked to be very challenging. To have points of supply and a place to stay with WiFi or cell service would require either a very short ride or a very long one. You can imagine which I planned to do.

I called the Siesta Motel in Havre owned by three sisters and got a good price on a room if I could make the 100-plus miles ride, with only very small towns along the way. One of the sisters promised to hold me a room if I promised to call and let them know if for some reason I was not coming. A large softball tournament was in town there, she said, and rooms were likely to be filled. Plus the motel owner promised me an "all flat" ride, making me optimistic that there was finally some smoother ground on the horizon.

Leaving Shelby, it was just me and the trains. I couldn't ask for more. Even though the mean hill I encountered right away was not quite what I expected, the terrain settled down quickly. Small towns I rode through with grain elevators and a few houses included Dunkirk, Devon, Galata and Lothair. All the towns and the tracks were on my left or north side, which I first thought was odd but the tracks service the grain elevators and the tracks were easier to lay in a straight line.

The first town of any size was Chester, my source for major fuel of two egg and cheese biscuits and a big bag of cookies. I had promised myself not to stop at all the historical markers and to take so many pictures, hoping for a faster ride. As you probably guessed, it didn't take me long to change my mind. I didn't miss a single historical marker with one of the most interesting being right out of Chester. The Baker Massacre in 1870 was a cold-blooded killing of 173 Blackfeet Indians by the U.S. Army. The soldiers, under Colonel Baker, were actually looking for another band of Indians which had killed a ranch owner the year before.

As I continued riding, a rather nondescript sign announced "Sweetgrass Hills," which I had not heard of or read about before. I kept riding into these beautiful rolling hills, a series of long grades considered sacred to the Black-feet. They used them for hunting and watching for enemies. The hills slowed my pace considerably but once I had made it past them, the terrain calmed down and I made better time.

Next came a series of lookalike very small towns, all of them with grain elevators galore. Joplin, Inverness, Rud-yard, Hingham, Glidford and Kremlin (the town sign said "the USA version") all looked to be almost totally agricul-turally dependent. I had plenty of supplies so I didn't stop at any of them. Between Glidford and Kremlin, I encountered a series of challenging hills and rumble strips that took the whole road shoulder. I was forced to ride in the road but minimal traffic and considerate drivers made it easy. U.S. 2 was a decent road otherwise, and the rumble strips only lasted a short time.

I made it rather easily to Havre, my destination for the night. Havre is bigger than Shelby and also has another BNSF switching yard. This one was right in front of the motel and perfect for my enjoyment. All the train activity along U.S. 2 was called the Hi-Line. The town was origi-nally called Bullhook Bottoms and was changed to Havre because of a large French influence. A wonderful IGA gro-cery store had everything, and I tried to eat a good portion of the store's contents. Havre will be worth a return visit for several reasons. Over a hundred years ago, an underground city was built and included a brothel, places to break prohibition without getting caught, opium dens and other illicit businesses. Sidewalks in town have skylights for the underground city built into them.

I got to Havre too late to tour it and hated I missed it. I think the underground city closed at 5 p.m., and I pulled into town just 10 minutes before. Close by is the U.S. Army Fort Assinniboine that served the area during Indian conflicts. Also nearby is an area where the Indians ran buffalo off a cliff to kill them in order to process virtually every bit of the animal for their subsistence. Over 2,000 years old, the buffalo jump was first used in prehistoric times because the Indians did not then have use of horses. The Great Plains area was home to possibly hundreds of thousands of buffalo until the European and American hunters nearly wiped them out in the 1880s.

The Siesta Motel was wonderful and the owner finally gave me a Montana map, my first ever after all my previous attempts to get one. The sister who told me that the route was flat wasn't working that night so I didn't get to discuss our different perceptions of "flat" with her but I am sure it would have been humorous. The softball tournament did fill up the motel and it appeared that all of the nearby motels were also full. This was another of those great days for which I ride!

Awakened by train horns, I was out early and back on U.S. 2 toward Malta. It was cold again, about 41 degrees. Havre has about 10,000 residents and lots of cars were buzzing around early on Saturday morning, maybe people on their way to that softball tournament. Train workers were also busy early as the sun came close to rising.

The next town was Chinook, near where Chief Joseph and the Nez Perce Indians were defeated in a five-day siege in 1877 called Bears Paw Battle. Chief Joseph said afterwards, "From where the sun now stands, I will fight no more forever!"

An easy to miss sign pointed to the next town of Zurich but I didn't see it, the sign or the town. Harlem was only big enough to have a busy convenience store. I saw that it also included a deli and asked about a breakfast burrito. The lady making them snapped, "Breakfast is over at 10!" After a pause and no response from me, she told me that she would make it anyway. It's a good thing, she didn't have any other orders and I only missed 10 a.m. by 5 minutes.

I rode past Fort Belknap Agency, a tribal center for the Assinaboine and Gros Ventre Indians, on my way to Dodson. It was a sleepy Sunday in the town, where I found nothing moving and only one little store open, which had very little inventory. I went in anyway and met a very gracious older man who I suspect ran the store more because it was needed in town than to make a profit. He talked about the town's lack of rain, the lingering heat and making hay soon. It wasn't really hot that day but it was getting warm. Huge hay fields ran in every direction and I expected that lots of hay baling would happen over the next few days. This was definitely hay country.

Possibly one of the reasons that nobody seemed to be outside was the horde of aggressive mosquitoes. I was attacked by them just past Dodson and at times, slapped five at a time. I kept "riding and slapping" for 25 miles into Malta, but never fast enough to get away from them completely. It's a good thing that the terrain had finally become mostly flat. I understood that the onslaught would continue past Malta.

Riding 90 miles on this day got me to Malta, and the first thing I wanted was a Dairy Queen milkshake. I got it, too, and then added another later. Malta was famous for having the fourth largest dinosaur skeleton ever found from about 77 million years ago, but I was more impressed by the trains and grain elevators. Part of Butch Cassidy and the Sundance Kid's gang — headed up by Kid Curry — had pulled off Montana's most famous train robbery near there. They got only a bag of gold coins and bank notes thought to be worth $40,000. However, the banks notes proved worthless, and the gang soon left Montana.

On my Adventure Cycling maps, I would find suggestions for motels that favor cyclists. I called ahead the night before to one of those in Malta and made a tentative reservation. When I arrived, the owner said I couldn't take the bike into the room. He had the worst attitude of any person I encountered on this whole adventure, and I ended up going next door to the Sportsman Motel. After battling those mosquitoes on the way into town and getting a poor reception at the first motel, I was happy to get a better deal on a room. The price was so low that I wanted to see the room before paying, but found it perfect. It was unique, with a small kitchen just inside the door, then a combined bathroom and bedroom which offered the opportunity to step out of the shower and two steps later, be in bed.

My pedaling that day had been along the Lewis and Clark Trail, which I also visited in other areas on the 2013 cross-country trip. Montana's American Legion puts white crosses on red poles at sites where roadway deaths have occurred. I would see them and then wonder about the person and accident. Multiple crosses, as many as five at a time, made me feel even sadder about the loss of life. On certain roads, not often the busiest ones, the crosses were very sobering in their numbers. My thoughts then turned ahead to a very sparsely populated segment coming up over the next few days and the end of my ride on U.S. 2.

After a great night in the unusual studio room, I dreaded another battle with the mosquitoes as I rode away from Malta at 5:15 a.m. The wind was already moving gently early, something I had seen over the last two days. On those days, the wind gradually turned into a tailwind. On this particular Monday morning, the wind became very strong quickly and started to pound me in the face. When a strong headwind blows directly at me, the rolling thunder in my ears never seems to end. I always tend to duck my head hoping that the resistance will be lessened. My view of the resulting slow movement of the cyclometer adds to the pain. On this day, the small hills, mesas, buttes, berms and whatever else seemed unending. Only on occasion did the terrain seem to shield the wind slightly.

I found the very small town of Saco about 25 miles into the day's ride. I stopped to get two egg sandwiches at a local café that also sold nightcrawlers. I was the only customer in the place, and the operator seemed bothered to hear that I wanted to order something. Her focus was on a serious phone call about some legal issues. The breakfast was very good anyway, and I sat on a bench out front to eat and stay out of the wind for a few minutes.

I headed on to Hinsdale, where I stopped in a very modern convenience store. I talked with the clerk about all the mosquitoes and why they were so numerous locally. It seems that the farmers irrigate their fields, and the standing water was a perfect breeding ground. Even with the high winds, I continued to be attacked by the pests but in fewer numbers. The hotel owner the night before said that they are sometimes so thick that they appear from a distance as smoke or fog. With the force of the wind on this particular day, I think the mosquitoes that landed on me started out in North Dakota earlier that morning.

By afternoon, the wind force was as high as I remember facing. It was funny how I could recall the exact days of similar winds on previous trips, one to Fort Scott, Kansas, on the 2013 trip and the other was my first day in Kansas on the same trip. I was resigned to a full day of discomfort and a slow 6 mph speed. My neck ached from holding my head down so much.

One usual sighting was the Sleeping Buffalo Rock, a sacred rock taken from a mountain that resembled a buffalo, complete with markings that defined horns, ribs, eyes and backbone. The rock had been worshipped since the earliest of times and was moved to a park in Malta in the 1930s. The Indians thought the rock was unhappy there and moved it under a little shed in an isolated area along U.S. 2 where it was at last deemed to be at peace.

Arriving in Glasgow after 71 miles of torture, I still had to pedal the last three miles uphill. I knew which motel I was looking for but once I found it, there were no more downstairs single rooms available. Thinking that I must look very tired, the owner gave me a four-bed suite just so I wouldn't have to take the bike upstairs. The price was right and the room perfect, thanks to owners Doug and Sharon Adolphson.

Two other cyclists were also at the motel, having taken a rest day. I met them as I walked my bike to the room and found that the next day's forecast called for the wind to lessen. Both the guys sympathized with the way I looked and I told them, "You did not miss a thing out there today!" I learned that we would both be headed the same way when we left Glasgow. They had studied the roads and hoped for a long ride the day after their rest. I heard their predictions and hoped for a tailwind to make it possible for me as well. Another day like today would be miserable.

Glasgow was the home of an Army airfield used for B-17 bomber training during World War II. The airfield eventually became an Air Force base and was used throughout the Vietnam war. Glasgow was another railroad town on the Hi-Line.

I spent a little time working on my upcoming journey into South Dakota, hoping that a new contact would provide some insight into what to expect since I would be on my own without the cycling maps. I seldom planned this far ahead but Montana would soon come to an end and I wouldn't be in North Dakota very long either. Evening email exchanges with readers of the Post, both at home and online, often provided useful information for the road ahead. Reading them was usually one of the last things I did before going to bed, but they always offered items for thought early on the next day's riding.

I was back in my element of physical challenge and an onslaught of adventure. There was plenty more to come.

CHAPTER 5

Leaving Montana and on to North Dakota —
Experiencing a mega storm

I began to contemplate leaving Montana but still had some work to do. My evening in Glasgow was a short one as I turned in early. It was easy to choose the best bed of the four because one faced a window that had the most direct view of lightning associated with a short-lived thunderstorm. I slept very well but just a little too long, waking up about 40 minutes later than I had planned and quickly attributed my tiredness to the tough ride against the wind the day before. It was unusual to leave the room with morning daylight already present. On the way out of town, I decided to make this ride a shorter one and catch up on my rest and deal with some other issues.

Right away, I found my cellphone locked up and had no idea how to fix it. Of course, googling the answer was not an option. The phone situation stayed on my mind and I kept stopping to try things, which contributed to a slower pace. During my earlier rides, especially over the Rockies, I had no reception for days at a time. I expected poor reception and just went with it. Finding my way without use of the phone and Google seemed easy enough then, but this time it wasn't. Finally, I just put it away and figured to work on it once I stopped pedaling for the day.

Another headwind started building early on but was manageable at first. A change in its direction began as I started to pass the little towns along U.S. 2. Nashua was first, but I had no reason to stop, and the same with Frazier. Oswego looked promising on the map, but it didn't in person. I just kept riding, buoyed by two cyclist encounters.

Chris Rea was a student at Rensselaer Polytechnic in New York and left two days after graduation to pedal west. His destination was San Francisco but he had also planned diversions at Glacier National Park and other parks after being joined by his girlfriend. I met Chris early and the wind was still in his favor at that time just as it had been on the day before. Riding was easy for Chris but I knew he had his share of headwinds, too.

Shortly afterwards, I met a very interesting couple from London also heading west. Tarryn Wickins, originally from South Africa, and Bastien Tren Hoste, originally from Belgium, were following the Northern Tier route and had 40 total days to accomplish it. I forgot to ask about their starting and finishing points, but both cyclists seemed super fit and I am sure were very capable of making their deadline. If not for having to get back to work, they said they would have detoured down to Mt. Rushmore and interesting points in

South Dakota. Since that was my plan, I asked about what I might miss by not riding directly across North Dakota. Both quickly responded that if I saw the Teddy Roosevelt National Park near Medora, North Dakota, before leaving the route, then I wouldn't miss anything. Chris Rea had echoed the same sentiments.

Tarryn was a marathoner, and we talked briefly about the London and New York City marathons. Her next goal was to get entry in the NYC Marathon, and I gave her details based on my experience running four of them. Tarryn and Bastien were such a bright and cheery couple. I knew they would be successful not only in completing the ride but in their other endeavors in life as well.

Wolf Point ended up being my home for the night. I paid too much for a room but there were only two choices, the third having recently closed. Wolf Point had a few interesting historical notes, one of them being the town's name. Trappers once killed several hundred wolves and stacked the carcasses next to the water of the nearby Missouri River. Men on a passing steamboat saw them and coined the name that remains today. Lewis and Clark passed through the area, and the local rodeo was the oldest in Montana. On a more personal note, Wolf Point had an Albertson's grocery store, another chain that had become one of my favorites. I remember a quote from a Montana resident in 2013 that reminded me of this area. I asked her how far it was to the nearest grocery store. She replied, "About 70 miles, and we always go and often make a day of it on Saturdays. Our only other choice is the convenience store which closes at 7 p.m." All of this was so different from my own experience, and their joy at going to a real grocery store was hard to comprehend.

I had gathered enough material to make a shipment home, so I stopped at the Wolf Point Post Office, where Tammy Tonneson took the maps, brochures, receipts and some winter clothing I no longer needed and boxed it up for me. I always collect information about the places I see and the people I meet, saving it for later moments to sort through for use in writing my next book. Tammy was especially interested in my ride because she remembered seeing me on the road earlier that morning.

Anticipating a very long day, I went to bed early that evening in Wolf Point. I had no idea of the challenges that the following day would bring, including one of the most dangerous weather events in my cycling history. The extra sleep came in handy.

Needing to get in a lot of miles, I was on the road early. One of my most important and telling habits has been to figure out the wind direction within minutes each morning. This day, I felt a gentle wind from the south and noticed the flags agreed with my perception. On S.R. 13 out of town and pedaling toward the Missouri River, I encountered mostly flat terrain early and enjoyed the sight of a major bridge crossing the river. It isn't used anymore but was an amazing structure, just like lots of the old bridges that I had seen on Route 66 the previous summer.

Past the bridge, the road changed and quickly began to include "rollers," an up-and-down terrain that lessened the fun. My short-term goal was to make it to Circle, about 53 miles past Wolf Point. My direction was more to the south for the morning ride, now facing a southeast wind of building intensity. There was little new to see since I was already quite familiar with miles and miles of grazing land. It became another morning of riding with my head down and hoping that the next hill was the last one. The one and only highlight of the morning was seeing Nick Cattin and Spencer Birchfield of Waldo, Ohio, again, the cyclists I had first met in Glasgow. One of them asked, "How do you like this ride?" to which I replied something similar to "I've had better days." The miserable morning concluded with us enjoying lunch together at the convenience store in Circle. As challenging as the morning had been, the next eight hours would be some of the toughest I had ever experienced.

The three of us left Circle just past midday and turned east onto S.R. 200, similar to a left turn. I found the wind to be continuing at near the same intensity. Nick and Spencer talked about the big hill coming up but there were plenty of rollers ahead, too. I took their picture and got ready to begin a climb to about 3,000 feet when they spotted a couple of storm clouds way behind us. I told them, "Montana is like this often but the storms hardly ever cross that much sky.

We'll be fine." I should have kept my mouth shut.

As the strong headwind continued, I began to doubt if I could make the next 50 miles before dark. There simply was no place to escape the wind. Nick and Spencer pulled away gradually as the storms started to pick up speed. I noticed that a big portion of the western sky was now filled with dangerous-looking clouds. I kept climbing and stopped to grab a quick snack and a drink of water when I realized that the clouds had gotten very close and were about to overtake me. Suddenly, the wind became a strong tailwind, changing in just a couple of minutes' time. I got my rain jacket out and realized then that the wind was now also much colder. As the light rain caught up with me, I went up and over the last big mountain and was suddenly making good time with the strong tailwind. In just minutes, my outlook for the afternoon changed from agonizingly slow into uncertainty. With heavy rain starting to fall, I began to pedal into lessening visibility. With so much traffic on the road that didn't slow down, I was constantly sprayed by trucks and cars as the road began to have significant standing water.

I began to worry a little bit as the rain got even harder and hail also began to fall. I couldn't remember riding in hail before. Even with the heavy rain and hail, the lightning and wind became my biggest concerns. The whole sky had closed in with heavy clouds, something that a local resident told me later that she had seldom seen. The sky appears so big here that several storms can be happening at one time but huge pockets of sunny skies usually intermingle with them.

During the worst of the storm, the wind began to gust from the sides at irregular intervals. As the storm cells passed, the gusts would come from the left for a while and then from the right. Lightning seemed to be striking all around me. The experience was unbelievable but oddly I was never really worried because I was constantly praying for safety. Worst of all were the strong gusts of wind from the side that caused the bike to be blown sideways, either toward the edge of the pavement to the right or into traffic on the left. Keeping my balance was challenging when a gust would suddenly stop as I was leaning into it.

A friend later wrote, "Why did you not just get out of the weather?" That was a good question but there was ab-solutely no place to go, not a single building or an overpass. I had no choice but to keep riding until I reached Lindsay, the only other town between Circle and Glendive. Lindsay consisted of a few houses and one store, a sort of hardware/convenience store combination. The storm had lessened slightly, and there was no more hail. I stopped, hoping to see the other cyclists as I noticed two bikes parked out-side. They were not Spencer or Nick, but rather two guys I had never met. They looked shell-shocked as they asked me what I had ridden through. They were heading west and didn't have a place to stay. I used the bathroom and got back on the road, hoping to end the day as soon as possible.

I still had at least 20 more miles to ride, but when I got back on the bike, darkness seemed to be closing in even though it was not yet 5 p.m. Clouds were heavy and low hanging, and a strong tail wind was still blowing. I had a wide shoulder to ride on and immediately began to make good time. A few bright spots were piercing the clouds ahead of me, and I began to hope for the end of this battering. Little did I realize that what would happen next was even a possibility. Within just minutes, I was suddenly riding into a brutal headwind that was probably part of the clearing ahead. It was the strongest wind that I had ever faced, so strong that when I tried to pedal, the bike would barely move forward and was so slow that I could hardly balance. Two times, I was unable to pedal forward and had to stop. I realized that I was already exhausted.

I was now just about 12 miles from Glendive, but my progress was insignificant. Worried about what lay ahead, I just put my head down and prayed again right there. Five minutes later, the wind gradually began to lessen and my progress increased with about eight miles left to go. I struggled on into town with 104 total miles, worn out and hungry. I stopped at a Subway just before finding the room I had reserved at the Yellowstone River Inn, another great deal that I would only be in for about eight hours. Still, I was relieved to be off that bike seat and soon put my feet up. I couldn't have been more tired. Once my story was submitted, I actually thought about going straight to bed. I didn't, but few minutes were wasted before my head hit the pillow. North Dakota was just ahead!

One of the shortest nights so far passed very quickly in yet another great motel at the Yellowstone River Inn in Glendive. Too many nights lately, I would arrive just about dark and leave as soon as there was enough light to see and be seen. My motel search has always been a part of the big adventure, usually a source of fun and amusement plus some challenges as well. The actual search has always been based on certain criteria. Nearly every time, I start with trying to find the best price for a room close to the actual route. I remember once reserving a room for a steal of a price but when I got to the town, I found that I had to ride about seven miles off route to get there. To make matters worse, there was not a store within that seven miles, so thankfully I had packed some stuff in one of my bags. Long ago, I learned to ask about available food nearby but also learned that some motels think bar food was all a bicycle traveler might need.

I used motels.com and occasionally would click on Google or Yahoo for the town or area and see what was listed as available motels. One big lesson from that process was that motels which may have closed would still be listed. One time I kept calling a motel, the only one in the area, but never got an answer. The message indicated that someone would call me back. Several convenience store operators I asked along the way said that the motel was still open. When I got there, however, the motel looked in pretty good shape but not a car was in sight. There were no signs saying that it had closed either, but it was. I began to pay more attention to Yelp and Trip Adviser reviews after this experience.

Almost never did I book a motel by supplying a credit card number unless I was convinced that available rooms were minimal and that I had better lock one in. This only happened a couple of times on the average trip and even then, I didn't usually find things to be as crowded as I had been told. Often just sharing that I am on an extensive solo bike ride will get the owners or managers to give me preference. The absolute worst case scenario happened in Canada in 2015 when I left Owen Sound headed for Toronto. For about a hundred miles, every single available room was booked for a wedding. I found myself riding in near darkness with no prospects. But I also found a motel owner's wife who saw my forlorn face and jumped in to solve my dilemma. She talked her husband into renting me part of a suite that was already booked to another person who just happened to be away for that night.

These things used to worry me more than I should have let them, but lots of miles and days on the road have eased my worry. Something always seems to work out, and if by chance it doesn't, then my tent and sleeping bag are on the bike. Only once in just over 200 nights have I had a serious altercation with a motel manager. That happened on the Route 66 trip when a Day's Inn was the only hotel for many miles. I called and got a price the night before but was not given that same price when I arrived. The manager said, "Take it or leave it, I'll book that room tonight whether you stay or not!" With nowhere to go on a very hot night after 100 miles of pedaling, I took the room but blistered him on Trip Adviser for the practice of not honoring the quoted price, more for my satisfaction than anything else.

All in all, it is genuinely amazing how nice and cooperative these motel owners and managers are. They seem to love my tales of adventure, and sometimes on a slow night, they try to draw me into telling more than my time schedule allows. Only on a handful of times have I slept in a room that wasn't reasonably clean, although I did back out of one that had cigarette ashes in it, a dip in the bed and residue in the refrigerator. That made for a nasty conversation and an invitation for me "to get off my property!" That was the first time I had heard that much English from the owner. She screamed, "Don't ever come back!" as I left with my $40 back in my pocket and a smile on my face.

Not only have the people been very nice, the amenities of the rooms have been amazing for the cost. I've had awesome views of mountains, the desert, oceans and lakes and sometimes even been treated to fresh cookies and discounts at nearby restaurants. Usually the motels were quiet and not too busy. One of my first requests if one does look busy has always been for a quiet room. Another big lesson learned has been to never take a room close to construction workers who have been living in the motel. In good weather, they all sit outside and drink and get louder and louder the later it gets. Several times, I have prayed for rain in this instance. Motels with only one floor have been the best, meaning I had no steps to push the bike up and no heavy people walking overhead.

My favorite time of the day is late in the evening, after my story has been submitted, my food eaten and messages returned. The pressure is off, and I get to just reflect on the day and think a little ahead to the next. Though my time alone has always passed quickly, I treasured it more than it's possible for me to express. I seldom really watch TV or pay attention to it unless the weather is on. Nothing is better than sitting in a comfortable chair outside, thinking and praying, contemplating and relaxing. After all, in just a few hours when there is just a sliver of light, I'll be back on the bike again.

Once out of the motel, I found Interstate 94 just feet away. With few roads in this part of the northwest, I was about to ride on the interstate again for the first time on this trip. Nearly all of the western states allow bicycles to use them, and "Share the Road" signs are common. I stopped and took time to load my bags with snacks and water but didn't really worry about supply availability on this day. I also usually loved riding on the interstate because the roads were generally in good shape, and the wide breakdown lane never forced me to ride close to the cars or trucks. I do watch for debris, including anything sharp, glass, bones of animals and steel belts from tires. Traffic was light on this day as I prepared to leave Montana.

The first town I came to was Wilbaux. I got off the interstate just to ride through the historic downtown and found it quite beautiful and well-kept. About halfway to Wilbaux, I had an unusual experience. A truck driver kept blowing his horn as he approached from what sounded like at least a quarter of a mile away. Without stopping to turn around, I just kept pedaling. The driver never let off the horn until his wide-load combine passed by, a few feet away. I never even felt the need to pull my elbows in but was confident that the driver would have stopped should there have been a real issue.

Next was North Dakota, another new state for me, with a spectacular welcoming sign. After making my required picture, I kept riding past Beach, North Dakota, because I had no real reason to stop and there was some uncertainty as to how the rest of the day would unfold. I wanted to make better time than I did the day before. However, I did take time to stop at a rest area in hopes of getting more information. None of the other states had rest areas that were similar to those back in North Carolina. Of course, I had not been on an interstate on this trip until this point so that could have been the reason. What followed was one of the most comical experiences I have experienced on my bike rides.

This one reminded me of my search for a campsite in Yellowstone National Park in 2013. On that rainy afternoon at about 4 p.m., I was directed by a park ranger to call a toll-free number for lodging and campsites, so I did. When a man answered, I told him that I was on a bike and needed a campsite for the night. He immediately asked me twice about the size of my RV. He later suggested that I ride about 40 miles in the opposite direction to get to a site, and gave me as an alternative, directions to hike seven miles off road to a primitive site. It got worse from there when he told me that there were essentially no campsites left in the park and that I could be fined for stealth camping. The call amounted to a half hour wasted. The next major campground that I came to had campsites, and the owners told me they always welcome hikers and cyclists. It costs about $8 for the night. I camped next to the woods and signs warning of bears.

Now back to the rest stop experience in North Dakota. With a ton of questions on my mind, I planned to get some answers. Foremost was to find a reasonable place to spend the night because I knew that all accommodations were usually pricey around national parks. I waited briefly to talk with the employee on duty and told her that I was on a bike and headed to the Theodore Roosevelt National Park and needed a reasonable room somewhere on the way to South Dakota. I also asked her for the best route to head toward Mt. Rushmore and the other major attractions.

After some computer work, she came back and offered to help me make a reservation for $199 a night, which she assured me was a good price. I told her it was way out of my price range, to which she replied, "Well, that is a cheaper room for this area. I doubt you will find anything for less." That room wasn't going to happen. Next, she asked if I was interested in playing golf or going to see a musical. I reminded her that I was riding a bike and those things were not a good fit for this trip.

My next question was about the best route to reach the Rapid City, South Dakota, area. She told me my best option was to backtrack for eight miles and take some road south to that area. Backtracking on a bike is not a fun thing and I still had a good ride ahead to reach the national park, so I declined. I next asked about the national park ahead and how I could see the park and the Painted Canyon on the bike. The lady told me that the Painted Canyon was not part of the park so I told her that my information seemed to say it was. "No, that canyon has nothing to do with the park!" she said. Of course, it turned out to be a part of the park and just as with all of her other answers, she was way off base on this one. I wondered if she had just arrived from another state and rushed into her job.

I was in her line behind a couple from Statesville, North Carolina, just about 20 miles from my home, but I didn't know it at the time. I did get to use the bathroom while at the rest stop, so the time was not totally wasted. I was just miles away from going off the Adventure Cycling maps and starting to truly wing it. The next town was Medora, famous for the Teddy Roosevelt Park and a cultural experience tied to the Old West. I stopped and made a call to a motel I found online, just about 20 miles away in Belfield. The day was starting to slip away and I had begun to doubt whether I could spend much time at the park visitor center. My incredible senior pass once again got me entry immediately into the park while others waited to pay. One of the park rangers on my Route 66 trip suggested getting the pass last year, and I have been using it ever since. Some of the parks cost more than the pass, and the pass is good for the rest of my life.

The park itself was established in 1947 and encompasses 110 square miles in its north and south units. The CCC, or Civilian Conservation Corps, built many of the roads, signs and structures within the park from a base camp that operated nearby. Inside the visitor center, I watched a movie about the life of Roosevelt and how he came to visit the area the first time. According to what I learned, Roosevelt came to the Badlands area because he was in a state of grief after losing his wife and mother, both on the same day and in his own house. Roosevelt, first seen as something of a dandy since he was always dressed in the finest of hunting clothes, came to hunt bison while dealing with his grief. He became so enamored with the great outdoors that he played a huge part in establishing the American national parks system.

Most interesting, just outside the visitor center was Teddy's renovated cabin from one of his ranches. The park ranger who took us on the tour pointed out the unique features of the cabin and said that it was actually state of the art for the late 1800s.

Another park ranger told me that the driving loop around the park was 26 miles in length and invited me to tour it. I declined, thinking I had already seen most of the animals in the park and more buttes than I would have liked. About that time, Harry and Linda Johnson from Seattle walked over, and we discussed my ride, the bike and plans for the next few days. The bike continually started conversations, this one ending with lots of photos.

The town of Medora was founded in April 1883 by a 24-year-old French nobleman, Marques de Mores. He named the town for his wife, the daughter of a wealthy New York City banker. Earlier history of the area included a U.S. Army battle against the Sioux in 1864 and General Custer passing through in 1876 on his way to the Little Big Horn. A military camp was established in 1879 to protect railroad workers of the Northern Pacific Railroad. Custer was only a lieutenant colonel in the regular army but often was referred to by his militia rank.

Roosevelt first came to the area in September of 1883 and eventually invested in raising cattle by buying two ranches. The Maltese Cross was about seven miles south of town, and the Elkhorn was about 35 miles north. In 1901, at age

42, Roosevelt became the youngest president in United States history, serving until 1909. He called his years in the Badlands "the romance of my life" and often credited his Dakota experience with enabling him to become president.

Tom Mix, the great western movie star, was married there in 1909. The first "dude ranch" was established nearby in 1883. Medora had a rich history both as a cattle town and a mining center.

The town itself was busy with tourists, most of them walking around. I saw that the town had a confusing grid layout and went in search of Dakota Cyclery. I found the small bike shop with the husband-and-wife owners working and only one other customer. After picking up another tube, some CO_2 cartridges and buying what I thought were chain wipe packets, I rode away. What I wanted was a little towelette loaded with a clear oil meant to lubricate the bike chain by rubbing it all over the chain. The specific oil is meant to lubricate while not picking up grit. Usually after a week or so of travel, the bike chain needs lubrication to keep operating quietly. What I got was a cleaning towelette, for which I had little use. Cleaning the bike could wait until after it arrived home.

I left town, stopping to read some of the historical markers along the way, but focused on what lay ahead on the last 17 miles to Belfield. I knew the Painted Canyon was just ahead and was on the lookout for it, too. As almost always happens, the downhill into town from the west made for a huge climb leaving to the east. A quick call confirmed my room reservation but the motel owner told me to expect at least a couple of major climbs ahead. I don't know if he counted the buttes but there was plenty of climbing left and some construction, too. But honestly, 17 miles was a piece of cake by this time in the ride.

The Painted Canyon was actually viewable from the road or you could cross over and take an exit ramp to a larger viewing area. I just chose to stop and look several times toward the north. It was yet another beautiful piece of nature's work and definitely still within the confines of the national park. A brief rain shower and some smooth new pavement also highlighted my last few miles. Most of the day, I was the recipient of a tailwind and saw one cyclist battling it, head down and hammering, in the other direction. The wind had established itself as a major factor in how enjoyable each day's ride was. Today was fun. Who knew about tomorrow?

Belfield is not far from the famous North Dakota oil fields, source of enough congestion to steer Adventure Cycling mapmakers away from the area. From Belfield, I would turn south and leave the A.C. route for possibly a couple of weeks. The oil fields lay to the north.

Belfield was a small town, little more than a big crossroads. I stopped at a great convenience store and immediately engaged in several wonderful conversations. I asked one worker where the Cowboy Inn was located, and she told me and said to tell the owner to take good care of me. I don't think she gave me her name so I couldn't use it later. I loaded up on snacks and water and asked about a place where I could get some food. I was directed to a restaurant next door and enjoyed yet another conversation with a local cyclist while I waited on my "order to go." As my rides have progressed, I seldom choose to eat in a restaurant and never did on this particular cycling adventure until the front tire had been dipped to signify the end of the ride.

The Cowboy Inn sat atop a little hill, and I found it easily. The owner was waiting for me and said, "So, you made it?" I guess so, and what I found was one of the top five motels of the trip, one that cost a little more, too. Every room was decorated in a western motif and was extremely comfortable. One thing that I noticed about the western states motels was that most of them are still locally owned, much different than those along the Atlantic coast and Route 66 journeys. The Cowboy Inn had a unique feature that I had not seen before but it fits for the brutal winter weather in this area. To enter the room, you had to open a door into a hallway first, then open another door to enter your room. It looked perfect for quickly getting in out of the wind and elements and maybe even leaving a set of messy boots in the hallway before entering the nice room. More than most people, I love a high-pressure shower at the end of a long day, this one totaling 81 miles. I would head straight from the massaging hot shower into the bed, and I was usually asleep within a minute.

Out the door and back on the road early, I was quite chilly at 41 degrees. The Dakotas were expecting a heat wave and this sure didn't feel like it. I rode into one of the most unremarkable areas of my journey, this one little more than endless miles of pastures and hay fields. In fact, the area had been designated the National Grassland. It had very little traffic, few houses and few towns. I only crossed through one town during the day, and it didn't take long to pedal from end to end. Amidol, billed as the smallest county seat in America, only had 21 residents. On that morning, I only found one antique store open, nothing else.

I rode due south, except for one brief nine-mile stint to the west, and passed the highest point in North Dakota. White Butte was the name with an elevation of 3,506 feet. That word "butte" was becoming all too common, and I began to dislike it immensely. Probably a much stronger word would be more appropriate later.

This was a hard morning for me to get comfortable with just the right amount of clothes. With the tailwind back again, it was warmer and I stopped to take off my jacket. Randy Glettler from Regina, Saskatchewan, pulled over to make sure I was OK. Randy had been a cyclist, cross-country skier, runner and endurance canoeist. Randy didn't sound much like the typical motorcycle rider, and he agreed. "I am not your regular motorcycle driver at all," he said, "but I do it enjoy it." Randy was on his way to see the South

Dakota attractions and then he was going to head back to Montana, retracing much of the route that I had just taken.

Plenty more of the endless buttes slowed my progress as I rode on into Bowman, where I considered spending the night. After pondering whether to try for another 50 miles to the next real town, I talked to some local folks who had plenty of experience on the nearby roads. More buttes lay ahead, especially over the next 30 miles, so I chose to end the day's ride and looked forward to an early submission of my story. Not much was going to be in this report because the day's ride had revealed nothing spectacular over its 60 miles. I had started to encounter trouble shifting my bike in the low range of gears, which were not quickly slipping easily into the next one. There was plenty of pressure on those gears with all the climbing and shifting that was required to summit so many of the endless buttes. They might as well have named the state for them.

My room in Bowman was not certain because I had plenty of choices, too many in fact. I always wondered along the way if I had picked the right motel. Sometimes it was just simply easier to only have one choice. I chose the Budget Host 4U motel and received the biggest room yet on my trip, large enough to house a dozen people in sleeping bags. It was perfect for keeping the bike in the room but way more space than I needed. With plenty of time to plan and a hospitable manager who seemed to know everything about the Dakotas, I did a good bit of research and came up with a workable game plan for the next few days. I had to make it to Newell, South Dakota, the next day. For more than a hundred miles, there would not be a motel or campground available. The South Dakota state line was just 16 miles away.

CHAPTER 6

South Dakota — Mt. Rushmore and the Badlands

L eaving Bowman and back on State Road 85, I was concerned to see the wind blowing very early as a slight headwind. If the wind was moving at 5 a.m., my experience has been that it will likely be a big factor for the whole day. I just rode on and said a quick prayer, "No Lord, not that."

The road was great with wide shoulders and good pavement, and even very few buttes, as I made it to the South Dakota line and took my state line picture. It had been an easy ride to this point, but all of that had ended. Immediately at the state line, the road quality became very poor and the climbing that the locals had mentioned began. I was in my 41st state but not enjoying it much yet, and the stiffening headwind gave me even more cause for concern. The fact that there were no reliable shoulders caused a unique problem. The road was so poor that where the shoulders existed, they provided the best riding.

A cross between a butte and a mountain lasted for three

miles, ending with a Doppler radar and three cell towers as the wind began to push against me even more. With all that hardware on top of the hill, I thought maybe the worst was over for a while. Still the buttes kept coming and thankfully not much traffic because I often crossed to the other side of the ride to find the smoother surface. I passed even more cell phone towers and wondered why so many were needed in a state with comparatively few residents.

The small oil rigs that I had seen on previous trips began to be very common, more so than in the earlier western states. Probably less than half of them were actually pumping, which I attributed to the low price of crude oil this summer. That suited me just fine, and I noticed that gas prices were slowly receding as I approached the midpoint of this cycling adventure.

Buffalo, South Dakota, was next, the last real town that I would see for 60 miles. Buffalo was part of the Crow Creek Indian Reservation. I actually did find a motel there but was not interested. I had a long way to go on this day. One of my favorite convenience stores was right in the middle of the little town, and I just had to stop and load up. For once, I sat down and ate a couple slices of pizza inside and answered a few messages with the store's WiFi. The temperature was really climbing outside and the short break was nice. My bags were full when I left the store, and so was I.

Back on the bike, I received the best gift imaginable. The wind had shifted to a tailwind. Remember the group of residents who helped me choose to stop yesterday in Bow-man? They thought I would get a favoring wind and had as-sured me that the terrain would ease up some in the last half of today's ride. I bet they knew that the pavement would improve as well. Things started to click as I made much better time over the next 20 miles. Unfortunately, the new pavement did not last, and when it ended, I began to ride on some of the worst possible. Even the road was rough and the shoulders, where they even existed, were so broken that staying on the bike was a challenge. South Carolina and Kentucky had long stretches of miserable pavement, and now South Dakota had definitely made its way onto my list of worst cycling roads in America.

During this poor stretch of highway, I spotted a histori-cal marker sharing information of two significant Indian happenings. There had been a battle between the Crow and Sioux Indians nearby, and the Crows sought to escape by climbing the nearby buttes. The Crows had forgotten to take water, and the Sioux just waited for all to die in the ongoing heat. Also, the nearby "Canyon of Skulls" was cre-ated when many of the Sioux died after contracting a fever from the Crows.

Something I had been dreading was a crossover segment of road that I had to ride on to get to Newell. The farmers and a guy in the Buffalo convenience store had all warned me about this exceptionally hilly road. What I found was a wonderfully beautiful segment of the ride that did have some challenging hills. But it also had great pavement and long views of rolling pastureland, especially green for some reason. There was little traffic, just as there had been all day. I loved this little segment of about six miles, and the descent was made without seeing a single vehicle.

After a very long day and 109 miles, I finally found my historic hotel following an extra challenge. I had called and promised to stay at the Newel Hotel, built in the early 1900s, unless I let them know otherwise. Yet, when I called back upon reaching the town, the same lady asked if anybody had called me back. They had not, and I wondered what was up. When I asked for directions and told her where I was, she told me that I needed to ride back out of town and look for some street.

Thankfully, I realized that the street was in fact in front of me and found it, but I still couldn't find the hotel. The grocer who had just closed his store told me in which direction to go, but as I got close, I still did not see the hotel. Finally, two fire department volunteers told me that I was just a block away and made sure I found it. Newell is not a big town, but I struggled to make sense of the situation. Once I went in the door to the front desk, things progressed well. I took the hostel option where I had a room but shared a shower. This was a much older style hotel, similar to some of the others out west that offered hostels in 2013. There was a sink in the room but the bathroom was across the hall. I think only one other person had a room downstairs and was pretty sure that he didn't shower. Rooms with showers were upstairs. Speaking of those upstairs, I heard some floor creaking during the night but it was certainly a cool place.

After settling in the room, I still had to go find food. There were two convenience stores, side by side, back on the main road. I hopped on the bike and hustled over as darkness was coming quickly. I grabbed a few things but desperately needed ice cream. It was at this store that I discovered F'real milkshakes, one of the coolest ways to get a quick and economical ice cream treat. Informed later that we already had them at home, I was still glad to discover the automated treat. I just picked out a premixed frozen cup and put it in the machine, chose the thickness that I wanted and in about two minutes had a milkshake. My only complaint was that F'real doesn't seem to offer a pineapple flavor. Maybe they will want to sponsor me and provide my favorite flavor.

I rode back to the hotel, rolled my bike into the small room and sat down to eat while checking messages. It was dark outside and just about eight hours later, I would be back on the road. After a quick shower, I hit the sack after another very long day in the saddle.

Once again on the road early, I pedaled along S.R. 79 on a beautiful Sunday morning. After another stop at the same convenience store at which I had shopped the night before, I gave out my "best sign award" when I saw the owners' marquee. The words — "We use legalized marinara on our pizza!" — made me burst out laughing just as the climbing began. About the only early traffic was a dump trailer hauling manure a short distance away. I kept seeing him, headed one way or the other, totally sure that it was the same truck due to the unique odor.

I spotted a huge butte in the distance, this one called Bear Butte. I could see it for miles, and the riding got tougher as I slowly drew near. I stopped to snack several times as this was one of those mornings that I struggled to get going. My goal was Sturgis, the home of the world's largest motorcycle rally, scheduled for just 31 days after I rode through. Huge saloons and campgrounds dotted both sides of the road miles before I reached the town. Many looked to be preparing for the big week when the town of 7,000 would swell many times over.

In town, I was amazed at the number of motorcycles riding through or parked along the streets. Many riders and tourists just seemed to be hanging around enjoying the feeling of the place, similar to what I might do at Yankee Stadium or Central Park near the NYC Marathon finish line. I had been working to make sure to see so many local attractions that I wondered if it was possible. Sturgis was not far from Deadwood, the historic western town of Wild Bill Hickock and Calamity Jane. One plan I considered was to ride directly to Deadwood after Sturgis and then head back to Rapid City as quickly as possible.

Actually, I had hoped to do exactly this when I left Newell that morning, but with the slow morning progress it just wouldn't happen. I didn't want to ride an hour and a half to Deadwood and have to leave before exploring the town adequately. One way to get everything done was to park the bike for a day and take one of the of the many bus and van tours in the area. My goal was to get around to see Mt. Rushmore, the Crazy Horse Memorial, Custer State Park and Deadwood. After a lot of wasted time making calls with no reasonable results, I decided to head to Rapid City to take advantage of a fantastic offer from someone I had yet to meet but with whom I had exchanged quite a few emails.

A few messages back home to Leonard Wood, a world traveler with knowledge of this area, helped me to understand a few challenges that I faced. Now that I wanted to push toward Nebraska in a few days, getting to all my sites in a day was important if at all possible. Leonard told me about traffic issues and serious climbs that would slow my progress if I tried to do it on a bike. Just a couple of days before, Leonard had suggested that I call the Rapid City Chamber of Commerce and ask for suggestions. I did exactly that and received plenty of information.

Eventually, I heard from Bill Goodgion, finance director for the Chamber of Commerce and Visitors Bureau. Bill was a cyclist, mostly a mountain biker, and took plenty of interest in my ride. We began to exchange messages about the specifics, and Bill offered to work out a reasonably priced room through Airbnb. Now that I was going to make Rapid City on Sunday evening, Bill offered to let me use his car so that I could have an all-encompassing day sightseeing. I thought that was an incredible offer but wondered if finding a tour was not an easier way to do it.

After yet another call and more wasted time waiting on hold, I decided to give up on the tour deal and go with Bill's offer. Tour operators couldn't get all four sites on the same day, and availability was tight because I wanted to see these places during the July 4th week. Those operators said I was simply asking too late for them to come up with a good package. I knew Bill would offer suggestions on how to see everything in a single day and decided to make the best of it. Now, all I had to do was make it to Rapid City against a very stiff headwind that had continued to build all day.

My push to Rapid City was on Interstate 90, battling not only the headwind but unusual interstate rumble strips, the first time I had seen them placed all the way across the breakdown lane. The rumble strips were deep enough to have been very rough had I been able to go faster. The bike shifting mechanism seemed to be even worse on this day and I still had no idea why. I checked to see if any bike shops were open on Sunday in Rapid City and found none. Bill told me that Scheels, a sporting goods supplier, had an in-store bike shop and that it would be open. Scheels was on the far side of Rapid City, but getting the bike repaired was worth a little extra riding. Bill offered to pick me up just to make sure we made it before the store closed, but I was confident of making it on my own. We texted several times until I was sure I could get there, and Bill offered to meet me.

I did pass the Fort Meade National Cemetery on the way to Rapid City. The cemetery was started by the surviving members of General Custer's 7th Cavalry after the battle at Little Bighorn. It was named for Civil War Union Army General George Meade.

Rapid City has a population of about 70,000 residents and is the second largest city in South Dakota, next to Sioux Falls. It is billed as the "Gateway to the Black Hills" and was founded in 1876 by a group of disappointed gold miners.

I rolled the bike through the store and met the young operator at the bike shop. I told him the problem and he told me that I couldn't stay with the bike and would have to wait outside, something that I found very odd. Bill showed up and we introduced ourselves in person while waiting, until the operator asked me to come join him inside the bike shop. He told me that there was nothing he could do and suggested that the problem was a design flaw. Disappointed, I asked him to oil the chain and reluctantly rolled it back out of the store.

After yet another windy day, I ended up at the Airbnb room and then went to eat at Dairy Queen with Bill. After 59 tough miles, I submitted my story and set about planning for a big sightseeing day on Monday, July 3. Later, after two pineapple milkshakes and plenty of food, I spent the rest of my evening trying to understand the route and contemplating special things that Bill thought I should do. He suggested leaving extra early and driving to Mt. Rushmore first. The reason for starting so early was to see the sun rise and affect the color on the face of the presidents. Over the last few days, I had also received plenty of emails from readers suggesting more tips on making the best use of the day. "Don't miss this or that" was the theme of the messages, and I planned to see as much as possible. Often, I am consumed with the drive to see more than the average person can, but maybe that reverts back to the underlying theme for this and my other bike trips. I consider myself fortunate to have seen so many states.

Bill surprised me more than one time, once when he offered his car and the other when he suggested that I get up about 3:30 a.m. to allow time for me to be standing at the main viewing site for Mt. Rushmore by 5 a.m. Two constants on these trips were that I never seemed to get enough sleep or enough to eat. But I set my alarm to be up and out in plenty of time to reach the No. 1 attraction for this whole trip.

I headed out the door even earlier than usual to where Bill had promised to leave his car at the curb. I found a very nice sports car with a full tank of gas. Next, I planned to follow my Google directions out of Rapid City and head quickly to Mt. Rushmore. Signs everywhere seemed to be placed just where I needed them as I got used to the car. I was genuinely excited and happy to be able to use a car to see so much in one single day.

With only a hint of light in the sky, I pulled up behind a short line of cars at the gate of Mt. Rushmore just as a security person opened the gate. We drove in without anyone stopping us and I had one of the first 10 parking spots in a huge parking area, easily enough for what must have been a thousand cars. A few folks had emailed me and said that it wasn't necessary to enter the park and that I could see the famous presidents from the road. On this morning, I wanted to get as close as I could and the other early risers were hustling forward to a prime viewing area with a squared-up view of Presidents Washington, Teddy Roosevelt, Lincoln and Jefferson. In just a few minutes, the sun began to brighten and change colors by the moment on the famous faces. What a great call to be here! It would have been nearly impossible to do this by bike unless I had arrived the previous evening. I talked with many of the 20 or so people who were also on hand and was surprised to hear that quite a few are regulars.

Once the faces stopped changing colors, I was still in awe of the majestic site. I walked around for a few minutes and gazed into the windows of the museum. It didn't open until 8 a.m. and with so much to see, I didn't want to wait here with little to do for almost two hours. The carvings on Mt.

Rushmore were completed between 1927 and 1941.

Checking my notes on a projected route that Bill suggested, I decided to go to the Crazy Horse Memorial next. I found the entrance and listened to the specifics on an AM radio station, realizing that I had to wait almost an hour before I could get in. I checked my directions and decided to go to the nearby Custer State Park. Highlights included an amazing road called the Needles Highway with views of granite spires and quite a few one-way natural rock tunnels just wide enough for one car.

Signs for the cost of entry were posted often but when I came to the place to pay, no one was there. I wondered if this being the week of July 4th had something to do with it while others drove right into the park as well. Riding in this area on a bicycle would have been brutal, and I did not see another cyclist. Custer State Park had a famous buffalo herd that pretty much did what it wanted to do, often just stopping and laying down in the road. I never saw a single buffalo here or when I had passed through Yellowstone four years before. As I left the park on the other side, no one was taking money there either. Just another awesome thing about the day! It was now nearly 8:30 a.m., so payment didn't seem to be required for this day.

Back on the road, I headed again to the Crazy Horse Memorial. All of the attractions to this point were fairly close together. It was still before 9 a.m., and I was excited to see how far the sculpture on the huge mountain had progressed. I heard one lady at Mt. Rushmore say, "When I was at Crazy Horse last, the memorial was still not finished." I knew from reading about it that the work had been in progress for many years but soon learned that the end was nowhere in sight with only an estimated 30 percent of the work complete.

Crazy Horse was one of the Indian leaders at the Battle of the Little Big Horn where General George Custer and all of his detachment from a larger body of the 7th Cavalry were killed. Only one single horse named Comanche survived the battle. Crazy Horse never surrendered to the U.S. Army but they tried to trick him into walking through a jail door. When Crazy Horse would not enter, he was bayoneted in the back and died later that night at only 35 years of age.

The idea for the memorial began in 1939. A work crew was on site nearly every day of the year and plenty of major equipment can be seen from the viewing area. It was quite a stately monument when seen from a distance and my only regret was that I didn't take the opportunity to ride a bus to the top. An amazing Indian museum is part of the complex and was quite interesting, especially some posted information about the Little Big Horn battle. Plans for a future university about Indian culture were also posted.

Next I made the long drive toward Deadwood with highlights including passing through Custer and Hill City, both historical and touristy. Plenty of old buildings almost drew me in, but Deadwood was on my mind. Only a short stop for a huge brownie and some crackers in Custer delayed my travel to Deadwood, another town that I had been advised not to miss. I had plenty of time to spend the afternoon walking the streets. Parking along the streets was apparently prohibited and it seemed that any parking at all required payment so I found a $5 lot. The operator rewarded me with a coupon for gambling bucks, something that I didn't plan to use. I did find that the major industry in town seemed to be gambling and that many of the older hotels had been renovated, now with casinos on site.

When in just about any touristy site that offers bus tours, I usually take the tour and then decide what I want to see later. With several tour companies available, I chose the one that had been recommended by email from a reader. Right away, the bus driver told us that actor Kevin Costner owned the bus and much of the town. Once the driver's comic act ended and we got down to history, we learned that Deadwood was named for the drifting wood that piled up in the streets during a major flood. The wood formed something of a dam and kept the streets wet for quite some time until it was removed later.

The heyday of Deadwood was when General Custer, stationed in the area, discovered gold. The small, sleepy town became a boomtown in rapid order, once having as many as 50 saloons and 30 brothels. Tired of trying to find reasonable names for the saloons, the proprietors began to just number them instead.

Gold kept coming, and in fact, has never run out. Plenty of gold still remains in the area but the cost of recovering it has stalled any current efforts for mining. The Randolph Hearst family still owns a mine with shafts that go down 8,000 feet, more than a mile and a half deep. As I mentioned, Deadwood has turned to gambling and marketing itself as a historical town with plenty of interesting history. Two of the local characters who had lived there were Wild Bill Hickok, famous gunslinger and sometimes lawman, and Calamity Jane, known for her shooting, riding, drinking and other male-type things. She eventually traveled with Wild Bill Cody's Wild West Show. Hickok died from a gunshot wound to the head when shot from behind and Calamity, whose real name was Martha Jane Burke, was rumored to have drunk herself to death. Both are buried side by side in the town cemetery.

After about three hours exploring the town, I waited to see a reenactment of Hickok's murder before leaving. I had a front row seat in Saloon No. 10, very near the spot where the legendary gunslinger died. The actor who played Hickok took quite a while telling about the exploits of his character, how he died and then we watched it happen right before our eyes. Other gunfights were scheduled for reenactment later in the day and were posted so that the crowd would know where to see them. Also scheduled for most evenings was a reenactment of the trial of Jack McCall, Hickok's killer. Without cars parked on the streets, and with locals dressed in period clothing, it would have been easy to imagine yourself in the one-time boomtown during its lawless days. However, I doubt that the many historic motels ever looked this good in their early days.

Late in the afternoon, I drove to Sturgis and jumped back on the interstate toward Rapid City, the same road on which I had pedaled against the wind the day before. Bill had mentioned that the Air Force base also had a museum worth visiting so I checked on it and found that it had already closed for the day. When back in town, I rode by another bike shop that Bill said he normally used. My intent was to ask about the shifting problem but found the store locked up for the July 4th holidays. I stopped at a busy convenience store and loaded up on half-priced cookies and pastries, since it was past 4 p.m. Luckily, I have hit a few of those same stores on the bike over the years. With all the excitement of the day, I had eaten very little and began to do so immediately. I filled the tank in the car and returned to the Airbnb home, ready to make my report on an amazing day! Getting to sleep earlier was on my plan, too, since I had nodded off during the Crazy Horse movie and on the tour bus. On these bike rides, I have slept through portions of many historical presentations.

My thoughts turned to the Badlands just ahead and the last few days in South Dakota. Tomorrow would be another July 4th on the road, back on the bike again and headed toward a long-awaited special surprise. Thanks to Bill and Stacey, owner of my overnight accommodations, for taking such good care of me for the two nights in the Black Hills.

My legs felt good as I headed out of Rapid City with almost no holiday traffic. My ride for a while would be on S.R. 44. My mood was exceptionally good after such an exciting day yesterday. I knew this would be a long ride and possibly hilly, especially once the Badlands awaited me on the horizon. It was chilly to start but real heat was expected later in the day. Most of the convenience stores were slow in opening but I stopped at one of the last best ones as Rapid City began to disappear. I got some snacks and a topflight breakfast burrito that I had to eat right away.

I didn't know a lot about what lay ahead of me except that the few towns looked quite small. I used the little bit of information on the state maps and my ride director "OK Google" to see that the two towns coming up during the morning had a total of 31 residents. Caputa and Farming-dale both had stores but neither was open. I began to worry about my water supply as the heat started to build. Google indicated there was a store in Scenic, just a long golf shot off S.R. 44 and right at the beginning of the Badlands. I saw a car pull into the store and then drive away. No other cars were around so it appeared this store wasn't open either. I did not have enough water to make 31 more hot miles be-fore the next town. The first sight of the Badlands looked hot and baked to a crisp.

In an unusual twist, I kept riding past what looked like a railroad track. The little trestles and grading were all in place but I finally realized that the rails themselves had been removed. Also near the start of the Badlands National Park, I spotted large groups of prairie dog holes in flat sections. I had never seen this. Almost perfectly spaced holes, hundreds of them, had the little chirping animals climbing in and out and scurrying around. The chirping sounds from those with their heads up seemed to be some sort of communication chatter as I rode by.

Just a mile or so later, God took care of me again. A van from Wisconsin with two Asian women and some kids in it pulled over in front of me. The driver got out and asked if I could help her get back to Interstate 90. They had been riding through the Badlands and didn't know how to get to the interstate and head back to Wisconsin. I thought just briefly, "Wisconsin is where I am going, too!" I showed her my map and told her how to find it and then asked if they had extra any water. She threw open the van hatch, rummaged through some clothes and dug out a couple of bottles. I realized once again how things always seemed to work out. Just as with the spoon/fork saga, and memorable events from previous rides, God continued to take care of me. Lord, ride with me!

On my cross-country ride, I was headed up a very long and gradual climb through an almost desolate portion of a never-ending national forest. I had run out of water and although it wasn't really hot, I was parched and dry. I saw a sign for a rest area coming up soon and I thought I could fill up on water there. When I rolled in, the first sign said, "No potable water." I don't think I was hydrated enough to even use the bathroom. I knew that I had at least 11 more uphill miles to go and my thirst was uncomfortable. The biggest factor was that my tongue felt like sandpaper, and I didn't have enough saliva to coat it. I realized it was time for a prayer and said one.

This was a Sunday afternoon with very little traffic and none of it stopping at the rest area. The next person who pulled in, believe it or not, was a surveyor. How often would you find a surveyor working on a Sunday afternoon? I asked him for water and he said, "I normally wouldn't have any but I am in a friend's truck. There is a case of water in the floorboard." He handed me several bottles and I made them last for the next 11 miles until I reached a campground with a very small store.

Those two bottles from the Asian lady eased my mind and were just enough to last until Interior, my home for the night and source of an unexpected surprise. After 80 miles of enjoyable riding, I pedaled into the very special little town that was surrounded by Badland's mountains and proud of it. I looked for a store right away and found a very small one. Inside was just what I needed, ice cream and a Diet Coke, perfect for breaking through the dust. The clerk wanted to know why I was riding and asked if I knew how hot it was. I did not, but was informed that it was 103 degrees. It just didn't seem that hot. Google said it was only 98, still not much of a difference.

Each year on my cycling adventures, I looked for a rodeo, especially around July 4th. It seemed like every western town had a rodeo at some time during the summer but I had only found one in the towns in which I stayed overnight. That one was quite a distance away and didn't start until 8 p.m. This one was just a short walk from my campground and started at 7 p.m. Plus it had fireworks! I had to go! Kim Kerner told me that the rodeo was the oldest around and would probably have as many as 250 participants, many of them local. Even by late afternoon in the heat, many horses and participants were ready to compete. Everyone was friendly. It was going to be a special night.

I had a cabin reserved at the local campground. On the way to it, I saw a small concrete block building approximately 12x14 and labeled as "City Jail" and wondered if it still served that purpose. Just a few blocks away, I stopped by the campground office and checked in. I was greeted by a heck of a challenge just after I opened the cabin door. There must have been 500 flies in the 8x8 room. Someone obviously had left the door open for a long time. The cabin had an air conditioner but it struggled mightily against the heat. I went after the flies with just my hands. I didn't have the best success and needed help. I went back to the office to get a flyswatter, and the owner's wife said that many of the rodeo competitors had stayed in the campground overnight with their horses, and that's where the flies came from. I got some more water and some ice cream and also asked for a pillow and a sheet. Nothing came with the cabin. I gathered all of it and went back and ate the ice cream before knocking out every single one of the flies afterward. It was time for the rodeo to start, and I headed that way.

With only about 67 residents, Interior was alive that night with hundreds more visitors in town. The census of 2010 swelled that number to 94 but the population sign still claimed only 67. The rodeo cost me $10, and I would have paid more. The quality of the competition was very good, especially since the announcer reminded everyone that many of these guys and girls have used these same skills on local ranches. In the same manner as a knowledgeable crowd at a baseball game, these people knew what they were watching and cheered at all the right times. The rodeo announcer called the Fourth of July rodeos "Cowboy Christmas" because competitors could drive to several events over a 2- to 3-day period and find opportunities for more winnings. Rodeo participants on this night came from five states, from which he estimated that $77 million was up for grabs when all the purses in that area were totaled.

When these folks set off fireworks, they had a first-class operation. Pickup trucks and lawn chairs were all around town as people watched, with the first explosions timed to go off just as the last bull ride finished at the rodeo. Those fireworks continued for at least 30 minutes. A parade had started the special day earlier that morning.

Only with a little luck did I notice that S.R. 44 made a hard right turn at Interior. Since I had ridden through town to the campground, I had not seen the sign signaling the upcoming turn. Car lights illuminated the sign before and during the fireworks. I walked back to the cabin and found it much cooler as the AC unit had finally caught up. No more flies, thank goodness, and only minutes later I was in bed. I knew that the next day was going to be a long and sparsely populated ride.

Up early to an amazingly cool morning after such a hot day, I found the proper turn and headed south on S.R. 44. The pavement went from great to terrible at that turn, and road shoulders disappeared. Amidst a very colorful sunrise over the Badlands hills, climbing returned in a big way and for 10 miles of riding, I kept looping higher and higher until I could see Interior once again far behind and below me. This riding was not enjoyable and the only saving grace was that I could ride anywhere on the road because of almost non-existent traffic.

Finally, S.R. 44 made a left turn at a T-intersection back toward the east. The road improved again, and the difficulty of the climbing returned to more reasonable buttes and their numbing ups and downs. The first town, Wanblee, was a big highlight because I knew there was a store close by. Wanblee was a Sioux Indian town with not a lot of activity going on. I didn't see the store so I asked a worker at a very old church about it. He said, "Just a mile or so ahead, on the right." That was great news because I needed lots of supplies.

What I found was a super cool neighborhood store, quite busy and with plenty of employees. The store had some of everything, including hardware, plenty of groceries, a deli and so much more. My maps told me that I still had about 45 more challenging miles to go for the day and the building heat was an issue. I bought as much as much water as I could carry, a couple of breakfast biscuits and a baker's dozen of oatmeal raisin cookies. My bags would hardly close. Two store employees encouraged me to take it easy, drink a lot and take plenty of breaks. One even took time to come outside and wave goodbye as I rode away. There would be no more stores until my planned evening destination at White River.

The wind was insignificant but the heat was building. The highlight of the day was when Edna Kari of Kadoka, South Dakota, pulled over to see if I was OK. Edna asked if I shouldn't be riding at another time of day and told me to be careful. She left me a bottle of Lifewater and some popcorn. Her conversation and that Lifewater meant a lot to me as it did get hotter, and in fact, I used nearly all my water by the end of the day. This day reminded me somewhat of last year's ride through the Mojave Desert.

When I finally arrived in White River, the cruelest part

was two steep buttes that had to be climbed to reach the main part of town and complete 76 miles for the day. My motel was there, and I waited for the owner to arrive and let me in a room. Once registered, I went directly to the ice cream shop next door. I asked for a large pineapple milkshake and to my surprise, I was told that large meant a 64-ounce size. I ordered it and had completely swallowed the thing in 10 minutes. That was a lot of milkshake but it felt so good going down. Just 10 more minutes later, I was sick.

The last portion of South Dakota was coming and soon thereafter, Nebraska and Iowa.

CHAPTER 7

Leaving South Dakota, on to Nebraska and Iowa — Just past halfway

O nce my stomach and the remnants of the 64-ounce pineapple milkshake got around to agreeing, I was able to enjoy the comfort of another wonder-ful motel called the Thoroughbred in White River. My early morning ride was set to head south, again on S.R. 44. Yes-terday, this same road had pointed me due east but today, I would start off to the south. Early morning storms were in the area and the wind was strong, once again as a headwind. But winds driven by storms are subject to change and I had silent hopes that those headwinds would relent. It was al-most time for another sunrise over the Badlands, and I was especially glad to turn due east again to see it. The wind quickly became a side wind, trending more behind me the farther I rode. With the sunrise ahead, I anticipated watch-ing the colors of the sky and imagining pedaling into them.

I noticed on the map that the first small town was called Wood and within a couple of miles from there, I saw a most unique cyclist coming toward me. I was on the downhill side of yet another butte while Ali Cooper pushed her bike up the hill and into the wind which was strengthening even more. I had not seen another cyclist since turning south from Belfield and leaving the Adventure Cycling route.

I rode over to her side of the road and knew immediately that this woman was something special. She was older, hard to be sure what age she was, but the energy and youth in her eyes and lively speech quickly offset my first impression. We talked about her journey and just a little about mine, but it should have been that way. Ali was from Palm Bay, Florida, but had lived several places and had decided to go ride the country by bike and get to know people while sharing her faith in a big way. She planned to ride in the midwest for as long as the weather held out but wanted to be back somewhere warm by the time winter came. Already having traveled in Alabama, Missouri, South Dakota and other states, Ali was headed toward Pierre, South Dakota.

She was riding a beach cruiser that she had bought at a yard sale for $9, even though it was clean and still looked almost brand new. The sign on the front of the bike said, "Jesus the King." Her possessions were packed neatly in little bags that hung on the bike and she quickly pulled out her notebook to jot down important things that we talked about. Her bags were smaller than mine, just as my bags were smaller than those of most other cyclists.

Before parting, Ali told me that she had just talked with the mayor of Wood and had met him in an unusual way.

She said, "I kept putting my money in the drink machine and nothing came out. He walked over and got it going. I was glad to hear that somebody in government was such a strong believer in his faith." Ali suggested that I stop and see the mayor as I rode though. She traveled with only a Road Atlas, and what sounded like an older version cellphone for directions. I could have stayed and talked for a long time but we both had places to go. Ali promised to keep my card and email me when she was done. As I write this, I have not heard from her but hope to when the weather gets colder.

I didn't stop at Wood because I needed to get going, but did consider it when I saw the store where the mayor worked. Witten was next and I was almost there when I saw Sven Fischer of Germany pedaling toward me. Once Sven told me where he was from, I went ahead and used my one good line of German — "Ich habbe hunger" — which means "I am hungry." That is all I can remember from two semesters of German at Western Carolina University taught by Professor Herr Frank. I was always afraid he was going to call on me.

Sven and I laughed about how important that hunger line was for a long-distance cyclist. We shared information about traveling in each direction. Sven was cycling from New York City to San Francisco and was planning to take most of the summer to do it. After back-to-back meetings with cyclists, I didn't expect to see any more for a long time. None of the major cycling routes were anywhere close and only those with the super adventurous approach would even cross this area without maps. Both Sven and Ali seemed perfect to totally strike out on their own.

Just like Wood, Witten had less than a hundred residents and was the next town with only a mail carrier moving around. Next up was Winner, proclaimed by billboard to be the "Pheasant Capital of the World." Sven told me earlier that Winner "was a real town. They had a McDonald's and a Subway." Very few towns out this way had them. Bob Barker, former host of "Price is Right," spent time here as a young man. I rolled on through town and just as I was about to leave, yet another cyclist came toward me. This one was pulling a trailer, and he didn't seem interested in stopping. I was amazed to see so many cyclists in such a short time.

The rollers continued and actually got worse in the afternoon. A moderate headwind began to build and helped me become ready to get off the bike in Gregory, where the official high for the day was 95 degrees. I passed very briefly through small towns Colome and Dallas just before entering Gregory, a decent-sized town of about 1,300 but with no ice cream support. Hard to believe a town with about six places to buy gas only had one convenience store with such a paltry selection of ice cream. A hot ride of 81 miles made me really want some, and later, I was able to get vanilla at the local grocery store.

Yet another perfect motel for my needs just about fell

into my lap. After making a couple of calls, I liked the sound of the Parkdale Motel but didn't expect it to be almost out of town in an opposite direction. Owner Brett Oliver was a former truck driver and helped me tremendously with deciding how to enter Nebraska and then to push on toward Iowa. He also had some insight into finding lodging for the next night in a very sparse area. The Niabrara National Scenic River was just ahead, too, and I thought it must be really something to beat out the Mississippi and the Ohio.

With Brent's help, I was able to leap forward in the planning process and get some much-needed sleep. Just the day before, I could have easily nodded off on the bike. That would have been pretty hard to do with all the stimulation of the physical activity, the new scenery, bumpy roads and the amazing sense of adventure. The new sensation of being that sleepy on the bike could have been dangerous but it passed without incident. I got all my work done and took a fantastic high-power shower and lay down on the bed to watch a rodeo on TV. I saw the first horse come out and nothing more until I turned the TV off about 90 minutes later.

This was another motel with a unique feature. I had both a front door and a back door, allowing entry from either side. Most of my overnight accommodations only have one door. My ride had just passed halfway, and there was lots of planning to do, especially in the area just ahead that currently offered so little information. Memories were being made every day, nearly all of them good. Sometimes I don't realize how special a certain occurrence or place might be until later but I generally find myself riding along in amazement just about all the time. Just as Brett Oliver took quite a bit of time to pull out his laptop and explain the pros and cons of the few routes available toward Nebraska, other local experts often weigh in and offer insight that I cannot find otherwise. Add to that some of the advice that I get by e-mail from folks familiar with certain areas. Then I sometimes just say, "Now I at least know enough to get started." In fact, I use that saying more than I should readily admit.

On my way out of Gregory just before dawn, I noticed another unusual statue. Gregory promoted itself as the "The ground zero of pheasantdom." How could this be? Hadn't Winner, just 30 miles back to the west, already claimed the pheasant title? Gregory took the cake in patting its own back with a large statue of the pheasant on a huge base. It was even lit brightly at night.

Good roads and light traffic were both important as I made really great time early on South Dakota State Road 43, passing through a bunch of cool little towns including Burke, Herrick, St. Charles, Bonesteel and Fairfax. Two great egg-and-cheese biscuits, purchased from a grumpy convenience store checkout person, fueled a good segment of my morning ride. I knew that S.R. 43 would become Nebraska State Road 11 at the state line and it did just that at about 50 miles into the day. I quickly took a Nebraska state sign picture, at that moment registered as my personal 42nd cycling state.

I called ahead to another very small town called Niobrara, Nebraska, and booked a room at the only motel for miles. The owner sounded enthusiastic and definitely wanted me to stop in. I anticipated yet another discussion about how to best proceed east.

Almost immediately at the state line, the buttes returned in a big way. The first sign, the first town and the first county in Nebraska were all named Butte! I realized that this was going to be a serious state after Amy Epley back home emailed with the phrase, "Nebraska is not flat!" She was entirely right but I did pass through a lot more interesting little towns while mixing in the climbing. After Butte came Spencer, Bristow, Lynch and Minnow with a population of one. The best of all was Vergel, simply because I busted out laughing when I passed an inflatable snowman holding a sign that said, "B-R-R-R." Complete with sound effects, I could actually hear its teeth chattering in the near 90-degree heat. Vergel probably wasn't even an official town as I couldn't find a listing later.

Very little was noteworthy about this portion of Nebraska except possibly that I was riding along the Nebraska Outlaw Trail. I found that anyone can sign up to ride along on the 231-mile trail ride along S.R. 12, my latest road. I hope those horses pulling the wagons are ready for climbing endless buttes along with the camping and cooking required along the way. Nebraska was also green, much different than most of Idaho, Montana and the Dakotas.

A steep, elbow-sweating climb over the very last butte into Niobrara late Friday evening brought a big surprise. I had seen nothing of the Niobrara River, listed on the driving maps as the National Scenic River. Once I topped the last butte, I had a long downhill ride to a crossroad labeled Niobrara for the town, originally named for the river. Just before the town, I passed a huge bridge over a dry river bed of significant size. I stopped at the first thing resembling a business that I encountered. There didn't appear to be much of a town, and there was certainly no motel in sight. My list of questions was growing as I got off the bike to get some answers.

I was not sure exactly what the business was but it sold gas and a few soft drinks. I hoped it was OK to stop in. A nice lady set about answering all my questions. The river had been diverted and had changed the local landscape dramatically. The big Missouri River was close by, and she said I should see it. My motel was up yet another hill where most of the town actually was, and yes, there was a grocery and plenty of people. The lady then fired a long list of questions at me about my bike ride and how I happened to come to Niobrara. Before I left, she had arranged for an interview with the local newspaper later that day. One last thing — at the bottom of the hill approaching the real town, I could get no cell service. I was assured that would change as soon as I started climbing toward my motel.

As I continued on up the hill, the hidden town soon came into view. Niobrara had a car dealership, another sign of a real town, similar to those towns out west that had a Walmart or a McDonald's. I found my motel just at the top of the hill, where the owner was unloading livestock salt blocks from his pickup. No animals were in sight, and I forgot to ask him why he needed so much salt.

Niobrara was founded in 1856 and once had a fort to protect white settlers from the Indians. The major town festival each year is called Desperado Days. The Lewis and Clark expedition passed through the area in 1804 and met the Ponca Indians nearby.

I checked in at the Hilltop Inn and met the owners, Bob and Marilyn Janovec. Bob offered me an extra room discount if I would help him finish unloading the salt blocks. I said, "That works for me. Where do they go?" He just laughed and said he was about done. Once again in another room that more than met my needs, I realized that this room also had two doors, one leading into a hallway and the other outside. The town was very small with less than 400 residents. I asked for directions to a grocery store. Bob went through a set of elaborate directions, making me think it was quite a distance away. I tried to follow the directions and was about to ride out of town nearly a mile away before I realized it. There was no sign of any store.

I stopped and asked for directions from a woman who

was out getting her mail. She pointed me back downhill in the general direction from which I had come. I eventually found a group of stores and thought I was in the right place but didn't see an entrance. One more inquiry took me to the front door of a nice grocery. I loaded up on food, including ice cream, and answered quite a few questions from some very interested customers and people who ran the store while checking out. They loved the story of the bike ride so much that the manager asked, "Would you mind getting interviewed by our paper?" I told her that I thought this was already going to happen but left my card and phone number, just in case.

All afternoon, the driver of nearly every vehicle that I met on the road waved to me and all the Niobrara towns-people were very nice. I was impressed so far with Nebraskans and looked forward to the newspaper interview. Everyone seemed genuinely interested in my journey.

Feeling hot and parched, I made it back to my room and poured myself a cold drink and opened the ice cream. Before I could start on either, there was a knock at the door. It was reporter Valorie Zach from the Niobrara Tribune, asking if we could do the interview in about 10 minutes. She needed to go back to the office for something and wouldn't be gone long. We decided to meet at a picnic bench under a big shade tree on the corner of the motel lawn. I finished my ice cream and headed that way, just as Valorie drove up.

We talked in general about my ride and I provided the

standard answers, after which she started asking me about the mood of Americans in the areas through which I had ridden. She was especially interested in the farmers and how they were faring. The best question of many good ones was, "Do you think there is a genuine feeling of hope among the Americans you meet?" Of course I did and proceeded to tell her why, but then reminded her that I am very unlikely to meet those who are causing trouble after the election or involved with other unrest. One of my favorite themes since beginning the cross-country ride in 2013 was that there still was remarkable good in America, something that goes opposite what is often the focus of the networks.

After the interview, I went back to my room to eat the monster supply of food that filled my bags. Once the hunger of a tired cyclist had been addressed, I grabbed my map and went back to talk to the Janovecs again to get their thoughts on how to I should proceed in the morning. Marilyn was at the desk, and I asked her what she suggested. Bob soon came out and joined in as they pondered the question. Both said I should not miss the Missouri River and the beautiful bridge running across it. Marilyn said that local cyclists and some who visit often take the ride they would suggest for me. Bob agreed and said I should ride across the bridge and back into South Dakota and head east. Riding on the Nebraska side would be very hilly with not much to see. Considering this was the same advice I had received upon entering town, I decided to do it. My Nebraska swing would end early the next morning and I would use South Dakota roads to reach Iowa. This seemed a good time to trust the locals.

There was nobody out and about as I left Niobrara the next morning. I knew the bridge was just a few miles away, and I had hopes of getting to see a very special sunrise. Would anyone back home believe that I was headed back into the land of the buttes and poor roads and doing it by choice? Maybe the eastern side of South Dakota would be different.

I spotted the bridge from a mile or more away and pushed hard as I noticed the sun was just a few short minutes away from cresting the horizon. I wanted to take a photograph of the sunrise and sprinted to get it from the middle of the bridge. It felt good to ride fast on this morning and with seconds to spare, I leaned the bike against the eastern railing and got a series of great pictures. Sunrises, rivers and bridges were three of my favorite things! The Missouri was certainly spectacular here, and I could see why the locals love it so much.

Once across the bridge, I pulled into the viewing area and took some more pictures looking back toward Nebraska. What Bob didn't say and maybe didn't realize was that at least the first 10 miles after crossing the bridge was a long grade and steady climb up from the river. It would have been hardly noticeable in a car. As I pedaled upwards, I noticed several rain showers forming and eventually they closed over me with a moderate rain.

Just about 15 miles from the bridge after I had turned back east on S.R. 50, I looked to the south and could see the Missouri River far below. The full-time climbing had eased but a headwind had generated once I did turn east. At least I would have had the headwind on either side of the river but still I wondered how challenging the Nebraska side would have been.

I had the pleasure of meeting another cyclist who helped break the tedium of the morning. Marianne van der Weiden of Holland came toward me with a barking collie harassing her in the road. There were no houses close by but the dog had focused on her and didn't appear ready to back off. I yelled at the dog, and he seemed bewildered. Marianne was just two weeks into a two-month trip cycling the Lewis and Clark Trail. I asked her how the ride was going so far, and she responded, "It was rough in the beginning but is going better now." I told her to enjoy the tailwind today. By this time the dog had calmed down and was just standing with us in the road. We made pictures, and Marianne made a turn almost immediately to follow her maps with her new friend following right behind.

It was amazing to me that the three most recent cyclists I had seen were an older American woman, a young German male and a Dutch woman. While none of them were following the major American cycling routes, all had made a commitment to see the real United States. Over the years,

I had met some fantastic foreign cyclists and wondered if I would someday be able to visit their countries to return the favor. As of this writing, Marianne has returned home safely and sent a picture she took of me and the dog.

After leaving Marianne and the dog, I kept pedaling east into the wind. I even thought of just bagging the day early, using the extra time for doing laundry and maybe taking a nap. But that thought was abandoned because by the time I made it to Yankton both the climbing and the wind had lessened. I was determined to make it to Vermillion, the place that Bob mentioned as the next overnight point. Another positive was at least 15 miles of road construction where a two-lane road was being expanded to four lanes. With the new side still not opened to traffic, I was able to ride on the new pavement all by myself.

In Yankton, a modern-looking town compared to many of the others I had encountered recently, I stopped at the bike shop that was part of the Ace Hardware Store. One of my two water bottle holders had snapped a couple of days before, probably because of all the activity recently. I met Hunter Rockne, a distant relative to Knute Rockne, legendary Notre Dame football coach. I mentioned to him that I had been to Notre Dame by bike the previous summer and had pictures of Knute's statue outside the football stadium.

Yankton was the first capital of the Dakota Territory and was also linked to my visit earlier in Deadwood. Jack McCall, the murderer of Wild Bill Hickok, was tried and hanged here in 1877. Tom Brokaw went to high school here, and Lawrence Welk once worked in Yankton radio.

Earlier that morning, I had stopped briefly at a Casey's General Store in Springfield. I was in Springfield by mistake after having taken a wrong turn, but I was ready to stop for refueling. I was on the search for Twin Bings, a candy bar sold only in the states around Iowa. Casey's is a large convenience store chain, and I asked the clerk if she carried them. Margaret proceeded to tell me all about Twin Bings and even how she had tried to make them herself. Twin Bings, King Bings and Patriotic Big Bings were all made by the Palmer Candy Company, and I had been encouraged to try them. Margaret had only the Twin Bings but I bought two and only two because Margaret said, "They don't like the heat at all!" I ate one outside the store and the other a short time afterward. I had a new favorite candy bar and ate at least one a day until reaching northern Minnesota, which was apparently out of the sales region.

A warm ride on to Vermillion was all I needed to complete the day's ride. I bought a huge bottle of water that fit my new water bottle holder and pushed ahead from Yankton. The next town or close to one was Meckling, claiming to be the "Hay Capital of the Universe" and also said to have five exits. I only saw one exit so I have to wonder about the big title and how true that was. I had seen plenty of hay on this trip, and Meckling looked to be more average than universe worthy.

After securing a motel room for the night, I took time to check out my end of town. I walked across the road to a bustling convenience store, where I met Brittany Hanson and Tessa Musil, students at the University of South Dakota and more importantly, experts on the Bings. Brittany and Tessa introduced me to all three varieties, and I bought some of each. They also helped me to find the right driving maps for the area. I was just about 20 miles from Iowa and about to turn north. A visit to the local grocery and its deli set me up for the evening. I looked forward to a good night's sleep and more adventure tomorrow. The days were starting to wind down. Only 14 days of riding remained.

I did get that good night's sleep and left early enough to ride by street light. I didn't know much about Vermillion when I rode into town but discovered last night that the University of South Dakota has about 10,000 students and the town itself has about 10,000 more. Vermillion was where Lewis and Clark killed their first bison, and later John James Audubon visited there to study birdlife. Since nobody seemed to be up yet, I rode around the campus briefly and was quite impressed with it. When back on S.R. 50, I pedaled east toward another sunrise and soon came to Interstate 29. I saw a detour sign telling me to go one exit south and without knowing the reason, I didn't want to do that. My bike just doesn't like detours. After a quick stop at the huge truck stop at the intersection of S.R. 50 and the interstate, I looked at my map and decided to go one exit north and ride through Spink, South Dakota, and on into Akron, Iowa.

The short ride on the interstate went very well and I took the exit for Akron, looking forward to the photo of my 43rd state sign. I rode east into Spink, not much more than a crossroads with what appeared to be one dominant building and a few houses. Not a soul was moving as I took a few photos and rolled on. A series of very challenging climbs, known as the Loess Hills, came next as I met little Sunday morning traffic on S.R. 48. Finally, just a mile or so before reaching Akron, I expected to see the Iowa state sign. No such luck, I rode back a mile to make sure I hadn't missed it somehow. The South Dakota sign was in place for those heading west but nothing about Iowa for us eastbound cyclists.

Akron was just a quick right turn into another grain elevator town. One convenience store appeared to have lots of business, and I stopped to find a breakfast biscuit and check on the missing sign. While buying the biscuit, I asked the clerk about the sign. She said, "I don't know, it is supposed to be there. We also make our son get out of the car, and we take his picture every time he enters a new state."

I stood outside near my bike and finished the biscuit while engaging in two extended conversations. First I asked a guy buying gas about the best route north. There were two choices, and he suggested the older and less traveled one which did seem best. The other conversation was the highlight of my morning. The Brugert family — consisting of Jeremiah, Jerod, Josalyn and Kayla — was interested in my ride. Each of them had great questions about why I ride and the bike. Jerod added more information that backed up my road choice. I asked about the Iowa sign and they got really interested, saying, "I think it is there, isn't it?" I told them that I actually rode back west and still didn't see it. Jerod assured me that I could find one just up the road in Hawarden, similar to Akron except that it was just inside Iowa. It was fun to meet this young family as they were en route to church that morning. My last view of them was as they made the turn to go look for the sign. I am sure that if they had found it, they would have caught up to let me know.

My ride to Hawarden went very well and upon arriving, I stopped at another Casey's General Store. One man sat in his car while his wife shopped inside, and we talked about the sign dilemma. Just as Jerod had suggested, this man said, "Just keep riding north here and soon you will pass back into South Dakota near the river. You'll see the sign on the other side of the road." Since what they suggested was on my route anyway, I just pedaled on and quickly arrived at the river. You guessed it, nothing but a South Dakota sign. Once again, I turned and rode back south and still didn't find the Iowa sign.

Hawarden was one of the neatest little towns I had seen in several days and I was particularly interested in a collection of restored buildings along the highway that dated from the 1860s to 1911. The buildings were supposed to be open later that afternoon but I couldn't wait.

Based on my map, I had still another chance today to find that dubious sign. I would soon head back into Iowa near a small community named Hudson. When I reached the town, this time there was nothing on either side of the road. I checked the map again and found one last remaining chance on the next morning's ride and was confident to find it since that opportunity was on a bigger road.

I turned onto U.S. 18 and rode through Rock Valley, the only flat town of the day. Don't count this portion of Iowa as flat as it definitely was not. Maybe Minnesota and Wisconsin would be the two 100% flat states. I sure hoped so. After a quick convenience store stop for water and cookies, I pushed on to find U.S. 75, my route to the destination for the evening at Rock Rapids, Iowa.

U.S. 75 appeared to be a major road on the map, and I hoped for good shoulders heading north. My general direction for the next few days would be north so my plan at this point was to stick with U.S. 75 all the way into Minnesota and back to North Dakota. That's right, I was now going to leave Iowa soon and enter yet another new state in Minnesota. My northern goal before turning east was Fargo, the biggest city yet on the trip. And that elusive Iowa sign was still on my mind.

The quick left onto U.S. 75 brought me into the home

stretch for today's ride. More rollers but plenty of shoulder took me into Rock Rapids and the beautiful Four Seasons Motel. It was hard to choose between them, but in retrospect I will count the Four Seasons as the best overall value for a motel on my whole trip. I always look for a good price, a pleasant experience at check in, decent surroundings and of course, the room needed to offer the basics with everything working. At the Four Seasons, I got all of this and the room was exceptional. During my business travel over the years, I have had to pay three times the amount I was charged at this motel for a very similar room. Plus, as a fantastic bonus, the owner followed me to my room and presented me with an ice cream sandwich just as I rolled the bike inside after 87 hard miles.

Tomorrow will include my first ever entrance into Minnesota. Up ahead a few days, I hope to see the Roger Maris Museum in Fargo, North Dakota, and the headwaters of the Mississippi a couple of days after that. Then I will pedal on to my first encounter with Lake Superior, the largest and last Great Lake on my list. From there, I am headed to Wisconsin.

CHAPTER 8

South Dakota, Minnesota, South Dakota and North Dakota —
Chasing the good roads

A wonderfully restful night at the Four Seasons Motel was probably the best part of my journey to the Minnesota line. As soon as I opened the door on that Monday morning and looked out into the dark, I felt the wind. I was facing north and knew that most of my journey that day would be due north. A very early wind like this was the worst way to start my day. More than on any of my earlier trips, the wind continued to be a major factor each day. I could only remember one calm day since leaving Idaho. One reader back home said the wind always blows in Minnesota, and I hadn't even officially arrived there yet.

My plans for today were solid and looked good. Little did I know that they would go right out the door by midmorning. I got on my bike and walked over to U.S. 75, where I turned left to follow a short connector before the road turned right again and headed north. Just when I turned north, a tractor-trailer was parked by the road with its lights on. Once I started pedaling, my pace was only slightly faster than the truck driver's parked truck. It was going to be a long day!

First on my list for the morning was to find that Iowa sign. I had less than 10 miles to ride before reaching the state line but instead of taking the expected hour, the stiff wind caused it to take me almost twice as long. I did find both signs, an Iowa sign just as I was leaving the state and the very elaborate Minnesota sign as I was entering the next. The Minnesota sign was a full-fledged monument and actually had a well-worn path to it. I could only imagine that others followed the same ritual as me when they entered a new state.

Next came a very scary portion of the journey, something that I did not expect at all. U.S. 75 was a good road with great shoulders when I first encountered it in Iowa, but it was entirely different in Minnesota. Just past the state line, the road quality deteriorated and the road shoulder decreased in size. Dreaded rumble strips took up most of the available shoulder and forced me to ride in the traffic lane. Just as the road got worse, so did the traffic. About a third of the overall traffic was a succession of large trucks that already took up most of the lane. That didn't leave enough room for a bike, and as a result, trucks forced me off the road several times as I met traffic. The truck drivers apparently didn't want to slow down, and once I nearly fell due to the gravel shoulder beside the pavement. As several falls have proven for me, loaded bikes just don't stay upright on gravel. U.S. 75 was my intended route all the way through this part of Minnesota until I reached the Fargo, North Dakota, area. But with the wind slowing my rate of travel to the point of becoming a slow-moving road hazard, I decided to drastically change my plans.

I got off of the left side of the road onto the gravel and just simply walked the bike until I arrived at the next county crossroad, where I hoped to form a new plan when I saw it. There had already been several of these and they didn't look nearly as busy. I simply did not expect rush hour to be this harried so far from any sizeable towns.

County Road 270 provided me with an opportunity to turn west and avoid not only the heavy truck traffic but to turn sideways to the wind. Still without much of a shoulder on which to ride, I stayed close to the edge of the road and had little trouble due in part to much more considerate traffic. This was definitely farming country with a nice mix of cattle and hogs, and I enjoyed this portion of today's adventure.

The first town I encountered was Hills, Minnesota, and I thought a ride through downtown would help my situation in several ways. A local opinion or two couldn't hurt my chances for salvaging the day. Plus I was already hungry and a brief stop would delay my inevitable turn back into the ever-stiffening wind.

Inside, I found owner Orval Sundem and a few locals seated around a table, all of them pleasant and smiling. I suspected that Orval's store was the community-gathering point, and I listened to the problem solving going on as I gathered up a few snacks. Orv was behind the counter as I presented the items for purchase but he wouldn't take any money. He wanted to know in which direction I was riding and thus began a much-needed conversation about possible routes. We looked at my map and Orv told me what he knew about certain areas and pointed out which roads he thought had shoulders. His wife, Bonnie, stopped in briefly and he introduced her to me. Bonnie said, "We've been married 53 years, and I won't say all of them have been good." Then she smiled and left.

Orv thought my best bet was to work my way north toward S.R. 23 by using county roads 6 and 7. These were reasonably good roads but just hilly enough to combine with the wind for more challenging riding. To call this journey north anything less than a battle would have made it sound too easy. Just before reaching S.R. 23, I spotted a road crew filled with some "good ole' country boys." I asked about the roads ahead and realized that these county workers didn't have much more knowledge of them than I did after talking with Orv. One response from the county guys was, "Oh, there will plenty of shoulders on 23, but it will be all gravel." Thankfully, that didn't turn out to be true. Most of it had paved shoulders.

Just a short way down the road, I spotted dozens or maybe even hundreds of the big wind generators like I had seen in Canada in 2015 and Texas in 2016. It doesn't take a lot of research to identify these areas as places where the wind nearly always blows. These generators are so big that they are hard to describe. One source told me that the blades are 90 feet in length and make a "swooshing" sound as they turn. I once met a crew in Canada which installed the things. What a job that must be!

I turned onto S.R. 23, finding no shoulder at all but a much better road and very little traffic. I knew my bike would be OK in the road when I was almost immediately passed by a huge farm tractor that eventually drove out of sight without a traffic issue. The shoulder gradually improved and so did the wind. I passed through Jasper and Ihlen and finally rode into Pipestone, by far the biggest town around the area.

Knowing nothing about Pipestone at the time and glad to be nearing the end of a tough day, I was most worried about the quality of the roads in Minnesota. The first Minnesota Highway Patrol car that I had seen was parked in a median, and it immediately seemed a good source for more road information. After leaning my bike against a pole, I walked across the road to the driver's side window and waved to both of the officers in the car. The driver rolled his window down, at least most of the way down, and asked if he could help. I told both of them about my experiences that morning and explained that I was going to the Fargo area. My specific questions about the road quality and the types of shoulders seemed to hit a nerve. The passenger side trooper said, "Sir, I am sorry to tell you that most northern states have gravel shoulders and I believe you will find that all way up to northern Minnesota." I told them that gravel shoulders left no place for bikes to ride except in the road and heavier traffic made for unsafe conditions at that point. I said, "I don't believe anybody wants those dangerous situations to develop." The officer replied, "By the way, no riding on the interstates in Minnesota." I had plenty more I could have said to that, but they didn't seem very interested so I just thanked them and walked back over to get my bike. When I turned back to look at the car, the troopers had already gone and were out of sight. As an afterthought, I should have said something like, "With the conditions you describe, maybe the best place for cyclists is on the interstate!"

My total of riding miles for this day was only 53, and I was disappointed at that. The wind had calmed somewhat and it wasn't hot. I had big hopes for the next day. With the possibility of yet another return to South Dakota and more use of the same roads that I had earlier condemned very real, I began to wonder if any government officials had read my harsh words about the broken shoulders and poor paving on the western side of South Dakota. It seemed that just a few hours later, I would be testing the roads of the state once again.

Pipestone was one of those cool towns that had a specific and unusual place in history. Unusual quarries from many years gone by had now been preserved into the Native American Peace Pipe Quarries and received a National Monument in 1937. Indian tribes had come to the quarries for centuries for a unique stone from which to make their peace pipes, a practice that still continues today. The quarries had also provided enough of the unusual stone for decorative use around the town. Signs listed it as both sacred and spiritual. Late in the afternoon, just after the park had officially closed, I rode the mile and a half from my motel to explore the area. It appeared that many others were spending some quiet time in the park.

I have already mentioned the Arrow Motel and need to tell the story about how I ended up there. Having no planned place to stay, it was just after my conversation with the state troopers that I began to explore possibilities. I made a couple of calls that included one chain, where my inquiry was answered with these words: "Best rooms for less." Maybe less than their own usually higher prices, I discovered, but not less than others! Fortunately, I found a listing for the Arrow Motel, for which a very cheap price was posted. I called and was given that price and found that it was still in Pipestone, only about a mile away. I was due to get burned because my string of motel finds on this trip had been simply just short of amazing. This price was almost too cheap, which can often be a tip-off to upcoming issues. I thought immediately about the WiFi and maybe some loud neighbors or basic amenities not working. The Arrow, however, turned out to be perfect for me. I love a quiet motel away from major traffic and people. The room had everything that I needed and was just down the street from a Casey's General Store so I had plenty of choices for food. The powerful shower and a nice TV were also pluses, especially on this night of the major league baseball Home Run Derby.

With the days starting to get a few minutes shorter, I was impatient to get enough light to ride the next morning. I made a wrong turn to head east on S.R. 30 where I immediately looked for the sunrise. About a mile into the ride, I realized that I needed to head west, not east. On this particular morning, I was headed back into South Dakota in hopes of finding good road shoulders again. My U-turn in the road left the sunrise behind.

As I headed west on S.R. 30, it occurred to me that I had not seen a cyclist of any kind in Minnesota. I had to ride in the road but traffic was light and courteous. Once I crossed into South Dakota again, the road itself immediately got better but the shoulder didn't. Following my driver's map, I turned onto S.R. 32 to ride through Flandreau, a town that was part of an Indian reservation with the same name. Flandreau looked progressive and clean, and the road immediately improved. I stopped at the convenience store and loaded my bags again, watching an ice truck unload while I ate breakfast.

Flandreau Sioux Indians planned to have the first recreational marijuana lounge in the nation during 2015 but eventually dropped the plan. The town was first settled in 1857 and then abandoned within a year due to Indian threats. Christian Sioux later resettled the town.

The road out of Flandreau was so smooth and light in traffic that my ride over to Interstate 29, the gateway to Fargo and North Dakota, went by very quickly. With only minor hills and no wind issues, I pedaled easily to Brookings, the first town after Flandreau. Travel became quite heavy around Brookings, largely due to major construction along the interstate all the way though the town. Just a few minor tight spots where the shoulder was totally covered with barrels pushed me into the traffic, but all went well.

Out of Brookings and on the way to Watertown, I kept riding the interstate and came upon a potential problem. The paving on the interstate itself was a smooth gray asphalt but I found that the shoulder had been freshly covered with a new layer of small gravel and tar. The tar looked so shiny that I was afraid to ride on it, thinking that the mix would stick to the tires and possibly sling the gravel against the fenders. A sign posted by the work crew said to expect this roadwork for the next 12 miles. I didn't want to have to ride in the traffic lane and decided to test just what the mix would do with my feet. After walking the bike onto the shiny new surface, I found that my shoes didn't stick at all. Frankly, I was amazed because previous trials with new tar had not gone well. Already on this trip, the little bit of new paving that I had seen had caused clumps of asphalt to stick on my tires and make me think of a tire going flat. The 12 miles passed without any incident or sight of the workers.

My water began to run low and I needed to soon stop off to fill up. The day's weather was near perfect and I actually thought of taking a side trip to see De Smet, the home of Laura Ingalls Wilder. Wilder wrote the "Little House on the Prairie" series, which I loved as a kid. The TV show was a big hit for me, too. Google told me that her home was 39 miles away, just too far to ride on this day.

My arrival in Watertown was just in time to get water and I thought about some ice cream but decided to find a motel in town and then eat later. So began a much different motel experience than those previously listed, not one of my best. I called several places in town which seemed to be priced right online. One stood out, incredibly cheap and with rave reviews. Surrounded by chain motels where I got off the interstate, I asked about this place at the convenience store. The clerk didn't know about it but did recognize the location. She told me it was on the other side of town, probably at least three miles away. While just three more miles doesn't seem far when compared to the average length of a daily ride, I often didn't want to ride that far through a town and battle traffic and stoplights just for a motel. Unless it was really cheap! I called the place and she said, "Oh, it's only two miles, right on the main road."

146

Along the way, I saw a Zesto drive-in similar to the one that we had back home for years in Salisbury. I didn't know that they still existed. In a less hurried time, I would have been inside in a moment asking for a pineapple milkshake, only to compare it to the Dairy Queen ones to which I was so addicted.

After leaving the interstate, I tried to follow the clerk's directions and must have taken a wrong street. Then Google tried to help me get on the right track and finally several guys at a car lot set me straight. The interstate exit seemed so far away once I finally found the place. Just short of four miles of riding but certainly a shorter route would have been the case had I gone to the motel directly. The Budget One Motel didn't look terrible from the outside, and I had certainly stayed in worse. I walked in the door of the office and began quickly to wish I hadn't. The "manager" told me that no rooms could be rented because her computer was down. She ran back and forth to her server and made a call and just kept banging on the keyboard of her computer. I said, "Why can't I just give you my credit card number and go ahead and get the room?" to which she replied, "Because I would get fired if I did that." This didn't make any sense to me, and it made less sense that she wouldn't take cash either. Time was ticking away while this craziness played out.

I began to doubt the quality of the online reviews and asked to see a room. Another worker, or possibly the boyfriend of the manager, I don't know, gave me a key to go see the room. It was adequate but not spectacular and newly remodeled like the reviews said. Back in the office, I asked her how long before she could let me have the room and was told that she had no idea. "Oh, I don't have WiFi either," she added. One of my favorite terms for bedlam is "Clown Carnival," and I decided to get away from this. I called another place that turned out to be yet another mile away from the interstate and headed toward it. For $5 more, I got all the things that I expected in a Travel Inn room but unfortunately, there were no food sources close by. My bags were full of things to eat so I settled down and watched the baseball All-Star game after 97 miles of cycling.

About 30 minutes later, a brutal thunderstorm with lots of lightning and significant hail hit the area. The hail was heavy for about 20 minutes and pounded the metal livestock trailers parked outside so hard the roar drowned out the TV for a brief time. When I first heard the noise, I thought the animals might still be inside. The weather alerts on my phone warned that tornadoes were possible for the area, never a settling occurrence. Thankfully, I was inside during all of this heavy weather.

I did get a chance that night to plan for Fargo and one place there that I wanted to see. As a serious New York Yankee and baseball fan in general, I had been reminded that the Roger Maris Museum was in Fargo and hoped to see it. Maris had played in the All-Star game four times and had been the one who broke Babe Ruth's record with

61 homers in a season. Fargo was about 45 miles away. Thus passed Day 30 of my journey.

I found a news and weather report very early the next morning and heard that baseball-size hail had battered the area and that there had been significant damage. The storm had continued until after midnight. and the result included lots of leaves and limb debris along the road back to the interstate. With the storm's passing, a weather front had changed the wind direction, and immediately I faced a headwind. I had no choice once again but to put my head down and pedal. A brief stop for a breakfast biscuit didn't help my expectation of impending misery much.

On a trip that had already included so many headwind days, I knew that the middle of the day would probably be the worst, and it was. The heavy thunder of the wind in my ears was unrelenting as I struggled to make any headway. So slow was my progress at one late-morning point that I just laid down in the grass beside the road. If it had been more comfortable, I would have taken a nap and hoped for better conditions when I awoke.

With only one town along the way, I stopped at a truck stop that seemed as much geared toward other vehicles. The choices inside were amazing with all kinds of food being prepared, including plenty of reasonably healthy choices. It seemed that every car was stopping at the truck stop and I almost turned into a car in the heavy traffic. With bleak chances of lessening wind, I sat down to eat outside and was not in a big hurry to get going.

I've mentioned before that I love to watch the side of the road just to make sure that I don't miss something good. For some reason, someone had lost a big pocketful of change as I found about $10 in various coins. All of them looked like they had been laying beside the road for a very long time. Most were quarters and I picked all of them up, including one that was bent almost double. The cyclists that followed me along this same road would see only smaller coins.

Next up along the way was the amazing Waverly Valley Rest Area, situated so that the entire property is an open overlook toward the Coteau des Prairies, or Hills of the Prairies. Those darn glaciers had been at work again and had carved out the area about 20,000 years before, according to information from volunteer Keith Lee. He said, "The Dakota Indians moved here about 1679, but tools and remains from as far back as 7,000 B.C. have been found in the area. From the overlook, the viewer can see about 40 miles." It has been said that the valley was one of the earliest inhabited locations of the Western Hemisphere.

Back into the wind, I continued plodding along at a top speed of 6.6 mph. I was being pummeled so much that I remember thinking that 6.6 is better than 6.4 or some of the even slower speeds of the day so far. This total day of riding lasted 11 hours to only cover 62 miles. Not my best day! The next day had to be better, no doubt much better in order for me to reach my goal of Fargo.

I pedaled to the Holiday Motel in Sisseton, where the owner told me about the never-ending wind in the area and that the forecast called for it to subside quite a bit overnight. Sisseton was about two miles off the interstate and my nearby sources of food were Subway and a convenience store. I had a huge room with a big picture window that did little more than let me see the impact of the wind that continued to blow during the night. When I got up that next day, my first morning prayer was that I would get some relief soon.

Still on Interstate 29, I pushed through lots of farm scenery that included reasonably good corn and hay crops despite the lack of rain. Hog farms were everywhere, too, easily recognized by the fragrant winds. My hope was to make about 90 miles into Fargo so that I could turn east and continue the journey into northern Minnesota and Wisconsin. It would take at least less intense winds to make this possible and by mid-morning, the wind did ease off slightly.

My goal of Fargo was so important to my 40-day cycling plan that I never stopped once for food, using up all that I had stashed in my bags, including two emergency Powerbars that had not been touched during the ride so far. It rained some, and the wind made 56 degrees seem cold. Unusual rumble strips that stretched across the whole breakdown lane about every 50 feet were nerve-wracking although sometimes I had enough space to get around them on the right side. If not, then I had no alternative but to ride over the strips. Not deep enough to rattle my teeth, they were only a hindrance. The only hills on the day's ride were those over railroad tracks and roads that passed underneath the interstate. Traffic was light all day, and the wind continued to ease off.

About midway to Fargo, I was surprised to find that my map had disappeared. It had started to vibrate out of my handlebar map holder a couple of times while I was riding over the unusual rumble strips, but I had just pushed it back in and kept going. I realized that it must have slipped all the way out, leaving me without a map for the rest of the day. That wasn't a big deal because I knew where I was going, but for that day only. Tomorrow would be another story.

I had no expectations of seeing any other cyclists until back on the Adventure Cycling route, just a day away. As I pedaled along through a construction and repaving area of Interstate 29, I heard someone calling out to me. Just coming off an entrance ramp was Bill Huckabee of Sweetwater, Texas. Bill was riding north from his home to Canada and was planning to take a different route back home. He had planned his ride for months as this was his first long-distance cycling adventure. It was interesting to hear Bill's perspective on his initiation into one of my favorite activities. We ended up riding into Fargo together where I had a room reserved and Bill was staying with a Warm Showers person.

To put this journey in perspective, I had left the Adventure Cycling route in western North Dakota and then found my way through South Dakota, Nebraska and Iowa. The last few days had completed the U-shaped return to the Adventure Cycling route with my push north through eastern South Dakota and into Fargo, North Dakota. From Fargo, I planned to turn east again while briefly rejoining the A.C. route before striking out on my own again.

Fargo is part of the Red River Valley, where melting glacial ice and dammed up river water formed numerous lakes. The fine silt that formed the lakes' bottoms became what has been referred to as "gumbo." Sandy loam covers the gumbo, which naturally holds water well and then becomes easily tillable even in hot and dry summers. The Red River Valley runs the length of the North Dakota-Minnesota border.

Like other great river valleys of the world, the Red River Valley was once a center of civilization, first frequented by the nomadic Indian tribes and then a group of Scottish highlanders. Trees hardly grow in the valley but the fine soil is hospitable for small grains such as wheat. Spring wheat works exceptionally well, and the crop has been said "to unite the area." So much of the local economy relies on wheat and other grains. Prairie grasses also do well and are quite nutritious to livestock. The Red River Valley receives enough rain regularly to produce these crops.

By pedaling on into Fargo during rush hour, I hit the biggest traffic challenge of the whole trip. The last few miles included multiple runs across interstate entrance and exit ramps. It was just simply too dangerous to keep riding through these areas. I just stopped and waited until I could run the bike across the ramp, where I would remount and ride to the next one. Fargo has an estimated population of 120,000 and is the largest city in North Dakota. It is frequently referred to as "The Gateway to the West."

Once I reached the exit for the West Acres Mall, I left the madhouse rush along the interstate and found my reserved room at the Grand Inn. More like a huge dormitory than the ultra-modern motel that I expected, I still had a good price and plenty of space in my room. On my mind immediately was the walk over to the mall and planned visit to the Roger Maris Museum. I was excited to see it and knew that the mall was open until at least 9 p.m., but was anxious to walk over and visit right away. I got directions from the desk clerk and immediately headed that way.

For as long as I can remember, I have been a huge New York Yankees fan, and Maris played with the team for several years. During 1961, he waged a storied battle with more popular teammate Mickey Mantle to see if either or both could surpass Babe Ruth's 1927 record of 60 home runs. Maris took the lead during the last two weeks of the season and was able to surpass Ruth's record by hitting 61 home runs.

Maris, Fargo's favorite son, was a quiet and humble man who did not seek notoriety though he had excelled in every sport he tried while growing up. Maris once said, "All I wanted to do was hit home runs, get about 100 runs batted in and win championships."

The museum was not what I expected. Relegated to a back hallway in the mall, there was nice display of Maris memorabilia but some of his most important awards had been stolen. His "Most Valuable Player Award" was one of them. One of the best things about the museum were the seats from Yankee Stadium that faced a screen continuously running Maris highlights. Besides me, the only other people there to see the museum was a couple, and there was not even an attendant on duty. Maris himself had requested that the museum would always be free of charge. I was glad to have seen it, especially just one short year after having seen Mickey Mantle's boyhood home in Commerce, Oklahoma. My bike rides had taken me to these special places and would leave them among my permanent memories.

On the way out, I stopped at the information desk of the huge mall and thanked the young woman on duty and asked if she was the one who had helped me a few days before when I called. I needed directions and ideas on a nearby place to stay. The one on duty that Thursday night was not the same one that had helped me earlier, but I had enjoyed talking with them both. The mall had a giant fireplace inside the front entrance, especially nice for those cold winter nights.

After hustling back to the Grand Inn, I submitted my story and bought some food at a nearby grocery store. I looked for a driving map but didn't find one, leaving myself in a bit of a quandary as to how to proceed the next morning. I wanted to head toward the Northwoods country and was especially focused on the headwaters of the Mississippi, surprisingly in a state park in Minnesota.

For the first time, starting about 9 p.m. that night, I didn't have any sort of a plan. After working through some possibilities and realizing that there were few good roads to the area where I was heading, I went to bed too late and still struggling to figure out how to get there. I woke up and went to the front desk and asked for a suggestion. Certain roads in the area were not bike-friendly, and all of the most direct ones had issues. The Adventure Cycling map was certainly a possibility but it looked too roundabout from my location, meaning quite a few miles out of the way. The guy at the front desk printed me out a route with no less than a hundred turns, something I just couldn't do. I got a map and some food and sat down to come up with a solution. After finishing my egg biscuit, I decided to just take the A.C. route and be OK with it.

God sent another angel to me just a short time later. Adam Heckathorn, who was driving a small bus, passed me on the street and had pulled over to wait for me. Adam was a large-sized happy guy and very knowledgeable about the area. He was also a cyclist and rode to work nearly every morning, even in the brutal winters. Adam set me on a clear path which eased my mind somewhat even though I was very late leaving town. He gave me his phone number and asked me to call with any more issues. One of Adam's friends stopped by and talked about how hilly the route was to Itasca State Park for a cyclist. He later admitted that he had not ridden that far, so I discounted the info, and my outlook brightened somewhat.

Adam told me about a special bike lane that I could use and I was immediately able to get on it. The bike lane was for both directions so my ride through the rest of Fargo was facing traffic, opposite of normal. Still things worked out just fine. Very quickly, I was back in farm country and passed into Minnesota.

CHAPTER 9

Minnesota again and into Wisconsin —
The land of flies, mosquitoes and Bigfoot

I t might seem odd that I passed in and out of several of the main states during this ride. I call it strategic planning, but maybe it was more about feeling safer and not being jostled off the road. I left the southern portion of Minnesota because the roads had virtually no shoulders and were busy enough to keep me out of the traffic lanes. When I entered northern Minnesota just east of Fargo, there was virtually no traffic. I hardly ever saw multiple cars buzzing by, and even then, it wasn't much of an issue.

This early portion of northwestern Minnesota was not especially hilly and most of the roads were reasonable. My early travels were on State Roads 26 and 14. I stopped in the small town of Hitterdal and shipped home another packet of material that would be used for this book. Corrine Moore was the postmaster and works at two locations. She sees cyclists coming by often, probably because Hitterdal is on the Adventure Cycling map. The town has about 200 residents and was named after a city in Norway.

It was tornado season when I was there, and Corrine told me about a recent one that had hit close by. She said some of her neighbors watched it from their lawn chairs. I wondered if maybe the wind that blew there constantly had something to do with the frequency of tornadoes in the area. It has been an absolute pleasure since day one of my cycling adventures to speak to post office employees. They have always been pleasant and wanted to know about my adventures. At least one came outside to take pictures of me and my bike.

The weather was nice on this morning, and I was starting to make good time when I noticed a woman parked beside the road just ahead of me. She waved me over and handed me two of the best bananas I'd ever eaten and an apple, too. Her name was J.D. Bare but she didn't want her picture taken. I was just glad she took time to stop.

The day was full of conversations, one at a small store where I decided to stop long enough for a snack and a few minutes off my bike. I was behind an older man in line who followed me out to the bike, asking about my journey and where I was headed. He described the road that I would see just ahead, adding that it would be hilly. He didn't recognize the name of the place where I planned to camp. I had already been told not to expect cell service there and since a local hadn't even heard of my anticipated overnight location, it became a mystery as to just what the Tamarac Resort was.

I pedaled east toward an area with lots of lakes, for which Minnesota is known. I was supposed to be camping at one of the bigger ones. Right away, I noticed that all the lakes in the area smell good. The water appears clean and maybe just a little fragrant. I had a strong ride all day, even though there was little special to write home about. The route that I followed was just right, thanks to Adam back in Fargo for his help. Just one more time that good advice from interested locals has paid off, and of course, the always comforting knowledge that the Lord is with me minimizes any concerns.

Unfortunately, for the first time in a few days, the mosquitoes were back and occasionally joined by horseflies.

My arrival at the Round Lake area and the Tamarac Marina Resort certainly didn't herald any excitement. Nobody welcomed me, and I wasn't sure what to expect. I found a high-end, members-only campground and marina. There was a lodge with a small restaurant and camp store. Some cabins, large and small, were located near the water's edge. I walked in and told the man on duty that I had called about a campsite that morning. He frowned and asked me to sign some papers. Nobody inside seemed very happy, surprising when surrounded by all the expensive RVs and boats. I was reminded again that the resort did not offer WiFi, and I already knew that cell coverage was very spotty. On one hand, I was fortunate to have a place to camp. No other campgrounds or motels seemed to be available. It was odd that there would be so few accommodations in a heavy vacation area.

It was getting late in the afternoon after my delayed start and 78 miles of riding. I had an odd feeling about the place as I waited for the manager to come tell me where I could camp. There were no designated campsites. She told me that they didn't have campsites but allowed occasional cyclists to come there. I had been told that I could get power and have use of the bathroom and showers. The manager took me to what appeared to be a maintenance area and told me that I should set up my tent there. I had asked about a flyswatter to help with the horseflies, and she reluctantly gave me one. The manager helped me drag a picnic table to the chosen spot. Mosquitoes were already out, and I began to dread the later evening and night.

I sat down to write my story for the day and decided to order a sandwich and fries from the restaurant. I noticed that many of the RV folks were coming by to eat while I sat at a table completing my work. Nearly done when my order came, I finished quickly and picked up some water and a few snacks for later. When I paid, I was told again that there was no WiFi available. Three pictures that I had already sent by cell connection were hung up in my iPad outbox. My first idea was to walk through the big RVs and see if anyone had unprotected WiFi that I could use. None did, so I asked one of the owners if he had WiFi and if so, could I use it? His response was interesting, "No, I don't have it but the resort does. They just won't let anybody use it. If you will walk over to the pathway down to the marina, you will have the best cell reception on the property. That is what a lot of us do." I walked over and within a few minutes, the pictures and story were on their way to the newspaper.

The sun was going down, a storm was brewing in the distance and the mosquitoes were getting more active. I set up my tent and hurried in, hoping to keep the pests outside. It was still hot and I had issues to deal with. The one shower available was inside a one-person bathroom, and I just decided to go brush my teeth and pass on the shower for tonight. The manager had told me that I didn't in fact have power to use because all the RV spaces had their own receptacles and that usage was billed directly to the owners. I asked if I could use the receptacles in the bathroom to charge my phone and iPad. The manager reluctantly agreed. However, when I saw the bathroom, with no shelf or ledge to put them on, I didn't feel safe leaving them there to charge. I did my bathroom stuff and headed out on a mission.

The RVs were all plugged into the power receptacles, just as the manager had said. I decided to find one or two that were not being used. If anybody questioned why I was scouting the area, they didn't mention it. I found an RV that looked unoccupied and had nothing plugged in. When it got dark, I planned to plug my devices in and then remove them before any sign of morning light. All of this worked out well.

Once darkness arrived and the devices were plugged in, I crawled into the tent hoping for a good night's sleep. It was still warm but not unbearable. There was zero breeze, and the storm had fizzled out. Even though I closed the tent fly as quickly as possible, and just as soon as I was still, I could hear the mosquitoes buzzing. A few two-handed slaps seemed to knock them down, and I was able to get some sleep. Up early, I retrieved my phone and iPad, packed up my tent, sleeping bag and other stuff while being un-mercifully attacked by mosquitoes. My exit from the place couldn't come soon enough. Only a few boaters were mov-ing as I pedaled away from the worst night of my whole trip. Goodbye Tamarac Resort!

I knew the area was sparsely populated but didn't expect it to be quite so dramatic. I did ride past a motel, where no one had answered when I called the previous day. It looked full anyway, and who would have wanted to miss my won-derful experience of the previous evening?

My first stop was at an unusual country store in Twin Inlets. I noticed a sign on the door that said "Restrooms are for customers only." I went straight to the bathroom and when I came out, the owner was staring at me. No one else was in the store. I went around and picked out a few things, noticing that nearly everything was priced higher than I expected. Without even a pleasant greeting or any eye con-tact, he added up my purchases. His sign on the register said purchases of $10 or more were required when using debit cards. Mine came up to something like $9.79 and I asked, "Is that close enough?" The owner replied, "Not a penny less! I lose money if it's less than $10." I picked up an extra item, paid and went outside and watched as three people on two motorcycles went inside and quickly came right back out. It was obvious that they had planned to only use the restroom and that the owner asked them to leave. The next guy got the same treatment. It must have been a hard way to run a store.

While eating my breakfast biscuit, I struck up a conversation with Sarah Price from St. Paul, Minnesota, who was there buying ice. She asked about my ride and I in turn asked her about the best routes for my ride to Duluth. We walked over to her vehicle where her husband, Jaye, joined the conversation. I told them the route that I had in mind and got their blessing. The Price family headed off to spend a day on the water, and I pedaled away toward Lake Itasca State Park, home of the Mississippi River headwaters. I had read that the park has Indian mounds and a nature boat that provides educational cruises. To me, the draw was the headwaters and I wondered if others would think the same.

As I neared the park, the traffic got heavier and the hills became much more challenging, just as the bike rider in Fargo had said they would. Still, those hills were much less of a challenge than others I had already encountered on the trip. I made it to the park, where I went in the southern entrance. Upon arriving at the guard gate, I was told to take the bike path. She said, "We are always free for cyclists. Just take the bike path because the traffic is quite heavy at times."

I immediately got on the bike path, but didn't care for the switchbacks and having to stop at all crossings of the main road. I could deal with traffic, so I got back on the main road and found it not as crowded as some other situations I had previously encountered. The ride to the Mississippi source included the last eight miles inside the park and I made it halfway before I had a flat. When I began having difficulty climbing a rather insignificant hill, I wondered what was wrong and stopped. A quick look underneath the bike revealed that the back tire was already about half flat. Horseflies and mosquitoes were attacking me before the flat and really went at my exposed skin once I pulled over to fix the tire. Stopping to slap them was going to lengthen the time of repair, so I just decided to work fast and let the pests have their way.

About that time a huge SUV pulled up right beside of where I was working. I saw a teenager eating a big cone of ice cream and wondered why the vehicle had stopped. Were they going to get out and help me? Changing the tube in the rear tire isn't easy because of complications that require unloading the bike, then unhooking the chain and brakes. Two teens got out and one of them, the ice cream eater, said, "So, she gave up on you, huh?" I replied, "No, I just have a flat." His quick retort was, "Well, I hope you get her fixed." They fished in the lake for about four minutes and then jumped back into their SUV and roared away. Once I got the tire repaired, it was great to hop back on and head for the headwaters.

What I found was that most of the people in the park were there to see the Mississippi get its start, just as I was. The visitor center was a very busy place but not nearly as busy as the actual source of the water. The Mississippi starts as an overflow from the huge Lake Itasca, just about 12 feet wide and barely moving at that point. I enjoyed seeing the source but enjoyed even more watching the strange things that people were doing. A large portion of the people were in the water, ankle to knee deep, and a few were even sitting in it. Some climbed on the rocks, but everybody seemed to be enjoying the beautiful scenery and cool shade. I took pictures, soaked up the scenery and then pedaled away to try to reach a good place for the evening. I still had a long way to go.

Just before leaving, I read a sign that said, "Here 1,475 feet above the ocean, the Mighty Mississippi begins its flow on its winding way 2,552 miles to the Gulf of Mexico."

I was ready to leave the Adventure Cycling maps again after following it for a few days. My goal was now Duluth, situated on the shores of Lake Superior. As late as 2 p.m., I thought I was going one way until deciding that another route might be better. The Lake Itasca Park was part of the

Paul Bunyan area and I could have gone north for some more exploration, but it was time for me to leave Adventure Cycling behind and find my own way for the rest of the trip.

Spending most of the afternoon on S.R. 220, I passed though Lake George and Benedict with a good tailwind behind me. Kudos to Minnesota for good roads with good shoulders because the traffic began to build as I neared a heavy recreational area. I passed plenty of smaller lakes and was still amazed at how fresh and fragrant they were.

My final goal for the day was Walker, a beautiful little town on Lake Leach which was part of the Lake Leech Indian Reservation. After a little misdirection, I found the Lakeview Inn, my home for the evening. Many times, I hear the name of a motel and something like "lakeview" is included, yet there is absolutely no lake around. The Lakeview Inn was just as advertised and I had a grand view of the huge lake without obstructions. Lots of fishermen had chosen the same motel, and I am sure they liked the casual setting as much as I did.

After unloading a few things in the room, I rode back to town to get a pineapple milkshake at Dairy Queen and then stock up on food at the fantastic convenience store next door. I enjoyed my milkshake while watching traffic and listening to a bunch of female motorcycle riders talk about their personal lives. I left with a smile just before sunset and headed back to the motel for a relaxing evening after 82 miles, a flat, bugs and another day of joyous adventure.

I hated to leave Walker early the next morning but I knew that it was time to get on down the road. About seven days remained in the bike ride. My early morning view of Leach Lake was quite different than the afternoon before. The wind-blown waves of the previous day had been replaced by calm water although I suspected that the calm wouldn't last. I pedaled east again on S.R. 200 and into a small resort community called Whipholt, filled with tightly-packed vacation homes overlooking the lake. I rode through and marveled at how close the buildings were, almost touching in every case. With short driveways, the one road was packed with cars with no place else to park. I did see and speak to one person who was out walking for exercise that morning.

Many of my favorite days on these adventures have been Sundays. I saw Mickey Mantle's boyhood home on a Sunday, and lesser traffic always helps. I make sure to sing some hymns on these biking Sundays. This morning was unusual because I got the news that one of my best friends had died the night before from a heart attack, and my riding took a sad turn. Bradley Eagle was not only a great friend but one of the biggest supporters of my bike riding adventures. Some of those hymns were accompanied by tears as I found comfort in the fact that Bradley would now be riding with the Lord and helping to watch over me as this and future rides progressed.

Just one small story about my good friend included Bradley's own motorcycle as well as my bike. I was on the last day of my cross country ride from Oregon to Myrtle Beach, South Carolina in late July 2013. Bradley had decided that he wanted to ride down to see the finish that would include my wheel dipping in the Atlantic Ocean. I had spent the night in Bennettsville and was about 50 miles from the beach when I first saw him. Bradley pulled over beside the road and told me that he was concerned about all the heavy beach traffic and the fact that there no real room for the bike. He was genuinely concerned and offered to ride his motorcycle slowly behind me so that I would be safe. This would have been extremely hard to do as he would have had to balance his big motorcycle at a speed of 10-12 mph. Still he offered. I told him to go on, assuring him that I would be there in a few hours and everything would be fine. And that is the way things turned out, and we were able to celebrate the long ride with a few days at the beach joined by one of my daughters and several other friends. Bradley, it will be good to have you riding along for the rest of my adventures!

One of my favorite towns was Remer, Minnesota, billed as the "Home of Bigfoot." Minnesota in this Northwoods area had few towns and roads. The big fellow was probably watching me as I rode through. A bigger than lifesize cutout of Bigfoot was posted right beside the town sign. References to Bigfoot were everywhere as I passed through the brightly colored and well-maintained town. One store was especially interesting to me even although it was closed on this Sunday morning. The sign touted Bigfoot gifts and even listed some of them on the building. I left there forever concerned as to whether the gifts were for Bigfoot himself or for Bigfoot enthusiasts like me.

Remer has a Bigfoot festival in July and I had just missed it by a week. Two of the activities at the festival were storytelling and a Bigfoot calling contest. Again, did Bigfoot families from all around the area attend or was the festival solely for enthusiasts? I left Remer with more questions than with which I entered, and it is definitely on my list of places to visit again. Local church services were just getting out as I pedaled away from town. A Bigfoot watched from a field as I pedaled away, keeping a safe distance. It was fun to imagine the real thing, even though he did look just like the cutout beside the town sign. Maybe that one was real, too, there watching over things until the Bigfoot gift store opened!

Two other interesting things about Remer included the fact that it was Al Capone's vacation choice and that a prisoner of war camp during WWII provided labor for logging in the area.

The next town I came to was Hill City, making me think that it was probably at the top of some big hill. While I did have to ride over significant rollers, the name for the town came from Hill Lake, which is located close to the middle of town. I made a quick stop at the one and only open store to load my bags for the afternoon.

I kept riding into Jacobson and found the Mississippi River flowing through town, the same Mississippi that was just 12 feet wide at its source and would later be more than a mile wide farther downstream. Jacobson was about a hundred overland miles from Lake Itasca, and the river was now at least 60 feet wide and deep and fast enough that walking across would be very difficult.

Minnesota 200 ended and I turned once again onto U.S. 2, my mostly friendly road from Montana. In some ways, I felt like the U-shaped portion through South Dakota, Nebraska, Iowa and southern Minnesota was now truly done and I was back on track to extend the amazing journey.

U.S. 2 was showing some significant wear as I pedaled toward Floodwood, self-proclaimed "Catfish Capital of the World." Both the road and shoulders were in need of repair and traffic continued to build. Once the road became a significant challenge, so did the wind. I was on my final turn toward Floodwood when I hit my first headwind since morning, and it gradually increased as I neared town.

I had called the only motel in town ahead of time and was told that I wouldn't need a reservation. The price was higher than I wanted to pay so I planned to negotiate upon arrival. With the wind blowing and 88 miles completed for the day, I was ready to get in the room and eventually enjoy a Yankees/Red Sox game until I fell asleep. The bugs could bite somebody else tonight, and I had encountered enough during the day to convince me that I didn't want to camp.

The death of my friend added a certain mental drain that I usually don't feel. It was going to be good to just relax for a while without a lot of other worries. I was already on the road that would take me into Duluth or at least into the general area, and no major planning was needed.

Upon entering the office, I was met by an empty desk with instructions to call a number for service. I did as requested and found that the desk clerk was currently cleaning rooms. She came to the office and another interesting motel stay was about to begin. The clerk told me that she was just about finished with a room that I could take but I asked about the price before committing. I offered a negotiated price which the clerk initially said she couldn't do, then she tried to call the owner. Not able to reach her, we negotiated further and finally settled. I had my room. Little did I know that this was the last motel for at least 30 more miles and I had no other real options.

Once inside, I was impressed to find one of the very best rooms of the whole trip. It was tastefully decorated with the best of everything. I turned on the TV and wanted to check to see if anything about the baseball game was already on. I found the channel listing and clicked on ESPN. Nothing!!! The channel was blank so I ran though the other channels. There was no ESPN. I went next door to where the desk clerk was now working. She told me that I could change rooms if the game was available on the TV in another room. Nice as can be, she was very helpful but found no solution.

I was relegated to trying to follow the game on my iPad, not much of a substitute. Food and a Wisconsin map were on my mind next. The clerk told me that a bar/restaurant in town served breakfast all day. I called and found out that they did but it would be 30 minutes before I could pick up my order. I rode over to the bar and expected to pick up the food and then check on a map at any of the three available convenience stores. My poor evening continued when I arrived and was told, "We haven't even started on your order yet." So I waited and eventually left with what I hoped would be a good meal.

The evening got worse when none of the convenience stores carried maps as I found out by checking them all. The map was not critical as I could get one later. I did load my bags for what looked like a sparse ride for the next morning. Back at the room, I realized that it was getting cold and my body was ready to take it easy and just make the best of the situation. With the tradeoff of always attempting to realize something positive in a trying situation, the room itself was spectacular! Probably the second best on the whole trip. The desk clerk told me that the restaurant next door had TVs and would be glad to turn the game on. Then she said, "But they close at 8 p.m." I told her that the game would just be going good by then but thanked her for thinking of me. The Yanks lost anyway, but I still felt that I had missed something important.

Tomorrow would include my entry into Duluth, another

of the bigger cities yet to come on my long journey. I also needed to find a bike shop to buy some supplies and wanted to see Lake Superior. Duluth was just 43 miles from Flood-town. Wisconsin was just east of Duluth and my 45th state would be in the bag soon.

Another great shower and a good night's sleep counted for a lot. So did the warmth of the room because I noticed it was very chilly outside when I opened the door. That didn't matter because the wind was not blowing and the cool morning felt great.

After about 25 miles of riding on U.S. 2, I spotted a store that advertised food, snacks and a grill. I had visions of an egg biscuit, but what I found were four guys already drinking at a bar before 8 a.m. I told them what I was doing and that the end of my trip was in sight. They were not really interested, and my exit was quite easy. A real store about 10 more miles down the road had a Wisconsin map and plenty of snack stuff. I called one bike store in Duluth and found out how to find them.

Leaving U.S. 2, I got on Minnesota 194 and then U.S. 53, cruising right to Galleria Bicycle in Hermantown. This wasn't the store that I had called but I realized that this one was closer and took a chance that it was the best choice. Brent Edstrom was the owner and took special interest in getting me through Duluth while seeing the best sites along the way. Brent's family had owned the bike shop for a long time and knew from a cyclist's perspective what would work and what wouldn't. He also gave me some thoughts on how to get to Green Bay but admitted that he was not sure what would work best that far away.

With my bike supplies, several CO2 cartridges and another tube, I rode toward Duluth and encountered heavier traffic. Brent's instructions and explanations turned out perfectly as I entered the downtown area. My first sight of the city with more than 90,000 residents was dramatic as I topped one particular hill and saw a huge panorama against the magnificent Lake Superior background. Duluth is the largest freshwater seaport in the country.

I wanted to see Canal Park, what one resident described as "where everyone congregates on a nice day like this." The day was beautiful and a little chilly, to me anyway. I still couldn't imagine seeing beautiful Lake Superior, the largest of all the Great Lakes, frozen over near the shore in the dead of winter.

I had picked up more food at a Kwik Trip convenience store and hoped to find a bench on which to eat near the water. For a convenience store connoisseur like me, Kwik Trip was an amazing place. I had never encountered the chain before and only stopped in because I needed to go to the bathroom and buy something to eat while at the waterfront. What I found was a parking lot absolutely jammed full and a convenience store experience like none before. The store was stocked with healthy choices and plenty of fresh baked goods, all at great prices. Since I was there near lunchtime, the store staff was announcing new specials one after another. Speaking of the store staff, every one of them was very nice. So positive and upbeat!

With a little help on directions, I found Canal Park and rode through downtown to get there. Duluth seemed much bigger than it was and had a certain "big city" feel to it. I sat on a bench at the waterfront, just as I had hoped, and ate a few things while studying my map. I watched people, one of my favorite things to do, as they did fun things like cycling or walking along the waterfront. Some, like me, eventually just stared out at the water. I asked two ladies on the bench next to me for suggestions on what I needed to see and how to get back out of town going east. They told me to see the Core of Engineers Museum and the unusual bridge but knew nothing about how to head toward Wisconsin.

I went to the museum first and found it very interesting. Ship lore and history from the Great Lakes is fascinating and I could have stayed there for the rest of the day. Highlights included an exhibit on the unexplained 1975 wreck of the Edmund Fitzgerald and mockups of what a sailor's life was like onboard ships 100 or more years ago. The living quarters of the different classes of sailors was most interesting.

A specific type of high-lift bridge known as the aerial lift bridge, built in 1905, was the dominant feature of the waterfront area. The bridge was affixed on both ends and raised equally to the height that was needed to let the boat pass underneath. I was told that the Duluth Bridge was the only one of its type in existence, however, I saw one that looked very similar in Burlington, Ontario, two years before. One of the workers in the area told me that the bridge had no specific time to be raised but that when it was, a huge crowd gathered to watch it happen.

The afternoon was moving on and I had a long way to go. My route out of the downtown area had already been described to me. I was supposed to follow the bike path, cross over the Bong Bridge and I would soon be in Wisconsin. That formed the simple version in theory. It didn't turn out quite that simple.

The downtown bike path was fun, sometimes part of the sidewalk and other times part of the road. At most places, it was clearly marked. Twice the bike path disappeared as it dumped me on the streets. I knew my general direction was good but the clear route to the bridge didn't magically appear. I stopped to ask directions of a bus driver who wasn't sure. He said, "Just keep going east. You will see the bridge." He gave me two streets that he said would merge into the bridge but was not sure which would be the best on a bike.

Another stop at a parts warehouse defined the route better as the bike path was nowhere in sight. Finally, I saw the Bong Bridge ahead and just kept riding. I ended up on a special bike ramp that was protected by a concrete wall as I climbed more than a hundred feet high over the water. The wind was a factor that high above the water and forced me to ride in the middle of the ramp. To do anything else would have pushed me against the walls.

Somewhere near the top of the bridge was the state line. I saw the Minnesota sign on the other side of the bridge but there was no Wisconsin sign!! I would have to look for one later. Either way, I was in my 45th state and happy to be there. Wisconsin was my final state for this ride and I had already spent considerable business-related time there. My experiences in Wisconsin had been very good previously.

Richard Ira Bong was named the United States "Ace of Aces" after his service in the Army Air Corps of World War II. His namesake bridge was spectacular and offered plenty of great views. Traffic was heavy and rushed while on the bridge. I exited the bridge at the end and found a roundabout that put me back on U.S. 2 heading east toward Ashland. Brent from Galleria Bicycle had told me not to miss the ride to Ashland and its views of Lake Superior.

Immediately I entered Superior, Wisconsin, and began my way through town. A stop at another Kwik Trip store gave me plenty of choices to fill the available space in my bike bags. Now a little more sure of what was inside the fabulous store, I bought quite a few things and took time to eat, too. Sue, one of the store staff, said Kwik Trip could be found in only two states currently but that the chain was growing at a rapid rate. I could certainly see why. The food was very good and priced better than in most grocery stores. I was pleased with the healthy choices the chain offered and hoped to find many more locations before the end of my ride.

The town of Superior continued for quite a distance. I stopped once to make some calls ahead to possible motels and had several good options, depending on how far I could ride. Much of U.S. 2, the main road through town, was undergoing heavy construction and four lanes had been reduced to two. Slow moving traffic was normal until I neared the edge of town and U.S. 2/U.S. 53 became a racehorse interstate-type experience. I was warned at Galleria Bicycle to stay off U.S. 53 but there was no choice at this point. Thankfully, I had a decent shoulder on which to ride. With only about 10 miles to spend in this superfast environment, I just kept pedaling. U.S. 2 turned to the left and I took it into a much calmer ride through little towns like Wentworth, Poplar and Maple. Maple was unusual in that the main street going east was very steep and long, essentially requiring my bike to climb over a major hill near an open convenience store.

At the same time, two things happened. Another cyclist came up behind me making very good time. I also noticed a fast-closing storm from behind that would overtake us soon. Forecasts called for hazardous weather for the evening and overnight. I had already passed several motel options but had one in mind when I arrived at Brule, about 12 miles ahead. With the storm closing in, I spoke to the cyclist briefly and told him where I was going. He was from

Alaska and was riding the Northern Tier, making me realize that I had briefly rejoined the Adventure Cycling map.

With the storm pushing me, I rolled through Blueberry and its old and dilapidated buildings, leftovers of a town that once was. A fortunate stretch of downhill helped me to make a quick trip into Brule, where I spotted the Brule River Motel. I stopped the bike, knowing that with luck, I could be inside ahead of the coming storm. That is just what happened. My only concern were the trucks of construction guys who had rooms around me. I hoped for a quiet night. With plenty of food, I didn't go out again except to get ice from the office. The rain hit and the construction crews weren't seen again either.

With only Wisconsin left, I sent my story back east and went to bed early. I knew that tomorrow would be a challenging day. My riding would be in the heavy Northwoods.

CHAPTER 10

Wisconsin and the end of the journey

O ne of the favorite nights of my journey was spent in Brule. Due to the rain, I never heard a sound come from outside the room and slept wonderfully. Still, and maybe because of a deeper sleep than usual, I struggled when the alarm went off. It didn't take long, however, before thoughts of my first day in Wisconsin got the cobwebs cleared, and I rolled on down the road. Still stocked from the day before, I didn't have to stop at the store in Brule.

My early goal for the day was Ashland, the town that the Galleria Bicycle owner suggested I see before turning away from Lake Superior. The ride from Brule toward Ashland had some long grades but nothing too challenging and once again the traffic was not a factor. There were so few times that traffic worried me that I could describe this whole ride that way.

The first town was Iron River, yet another place that claimed a special relationship with Bigfoot. A big sign on the side of a building proclaimed the sighting. I thought the little town was quite picturesque and stopped in at its biggest convenience store. It was time for breakfast, and I soon made another discovery. If the store has a Subway, then that will likely be the only source of fresh breakfast food in the store. This store had that Subway and since I was still a few minutes before 8 a.m., I was told that they couldn't yet serve me. I chose not to wait 20 minutes when the bike wheels needed to be turning. A prior discovery of the same nature happened with Hunt's Pizza. If the store has this sign, expect a good breakfast business and little hassle to get it. I saw this scenario played out time and again over my various rides.

Ashland directly faced Lake Superior, but from here the lake's horizon appeared to be more to the north. I was told that sunsets in Ashland were spectacular because of the unobstructed view across the water, obviously taking in some of the western sky, too. If traveling this way again, I will be sure to stop in at one of the many reasonably priced motels and enjoy some serious sunset watching. Those special sunsets on the other Great Lakes comprise part of my reasoning to eventually ride the circumference of the entire Great Lakes, approximately 6,000 miles.

Long and cold winters are common in Ashland, and large volumes of lake effect snows make spring seem far away. British, Spanish, French and American flags have flown over Ashland and eight different Indian tribes have

184

called it home.

My biscuit that morning came from a McDonald's that seemed to be a community gathering spot. I find it interesting that some of that chain's stores often have large groups of citizens lingering after their breakfasts, then focused more on lively conversation. My own choice would have been a Kwik Trip instead but the store in Ashland was still under construction.

U.S. 2 was my road of choice for the last time that morning and I hated to say goodbye. I thought of the better-known iconic roadways that I pedaled over the years. While not as famous as U.S. 1 or Route 66, U.S. 2 certainly took me through a good portion of real America. My regret at that time was that I had to leave the friendly road and not see the rest of it as it headed east toward Bar Harbor, Maine, which just happened to have been my starting point of the 2014 Atlantic Coast ride. One thing that I noticed when it was time to leave U.S. 2 was that the road seemed most about landscapes and spectacular scenery. From Seattle, Washington, to Bar Harbor, this road has a great story to tell. One day, I hope to see the rest of it.

A slow but still interesting morning was about to take a much different turn. I called about a possible room for the night in Glidden thinking that the distance was just about right, if all went well. What followed was one of my more challenging afternoons. I turned on Wisconsin 13 with a southerly direction and planned to follow it the rest of the day. Clouds that had been lingering most of the morning soon brought an absolutely pounding rain, complete with an ample dose of lightning and thunder. The heavy rain started about noon and lasted about 90 minutes. Although I had a dry rain jacket, I was absolutely soaked otherwise. Visibility was very poor during the rain and my available road shoulder was minimal. I don't ride with a headlight on the bike but I doubt that anybody would have seen me in such a heavy rain anyway. Those who approached from the rear gave me room thanks to my very good flashing red light on the pannier rack. This was the second hardest rain experienced on this trip, second only to the harrowing downpour just east of Circle, Montana. It's funny how those heavy rains remain memorable for years.

Just after the heavy rain finally stopped, I found a Road Closed and a detour sign amid some light flooding. The roads were very wet as I pondered whether to follow the detour or head directly between the signs onto the closed road. Never knowing how far the detour takes drivers away from the regular road, I once again chose the challenge of making it through on the main road. As I began to pedal into the construction area, operators of the big equipment were just starting to move again after the rain. When the first big road grader passed me, I looked at the driver and he just waved. Obviously, it did not bother him that I was in his work area. Mud was terrible, turned very sloppy by the rain. Right away, my tires began to spray the sloppy mess over the bike even though the fenders caught some of it.

Places in the road had torn up pavement, and some of it had gravel where the pavement was missing. I realized that I was in for a long ride in the mess. Workers on more equipment kept passing, with nothing but waves. Maybe they thought it was humorous that I was trying to cross the area but nobody tried to stop me. My thinking was that there might be a huge hole ahead that I couldn't cross. The muddy mess continued all the way until the end of construction, about six miles from the start. Traffic was taking the detour as I rode past another set of signs, this time back onto the regular road. Both the bike and I were muddy, the worst ever. No other place on all my bike journeys had been this bad.

After exiting the construction area, the big hills started again. I pedaled through Marengo, which consisted of a small group of stores. Next was Mellen, obviously an older and more established town. I stopped there and used an outside spigot to get enough water to clean up the bike. I knew that the chain would need some oil soon because a low grinding noise was just starting. Mud was not good for a chain and neither was a heavy rain.

Mellen had one special claim to fame. It supplied the birch to build Howard Hughes' wooden plane called the "Spruce Goose," even though it was not spruce. At the time, it was the largest plane ever built and was constructed of wood but with a capacity big enough to carry two loaded railroad cars.

Just as I was leaving Mellen, I found the worst hills of the day. It was a slow climb to get over a couple of them and as I neared the top of the highest one, out of the woods walked a black bear. It walked slowly until I stopped the bike in hopes of getting a picture. The young bear, the first I had ever seen, quickly ran into the woods. The bear sighting would soon become more significant.

I was passing through Chequamegon National Forest at the time and the hills had slowed my progress. Those hills quickly leveled out and I passed the Great Divide, where in this case the water on one side flows into Lake Superior while water on the other side flows into the Mississippi River.

Glidden was my home for the night, and I rode into town ready to get my bearings. I knew the town was small but I had no idea how interesting it would be. First thing on my agenda was to find the motel. Unable to find it, I stopped at the Bear Crossing Convenience Store, one of those special stores that seems to keep a small town running. Amy, who was working at the counter, invited me back later to get something to eat and pointed me toward the motel. There was an older section of town across the railroad tracks and that was where I was headed. A very steep hill leading to Shroeder's Motel took all I had to make it, especially at the end of 78 miles. I met owner Gene Frey and heard that two other cyclists had spent the previous night there. Another huge, yet very nice room with a fantastic price started my love affair with Glidden.

I unloaded some of my bag weight and headed back over to the Bear Crossing store. Amy welcomed me back and asked, "Do you want something to eat?" which was certainly a crazy question. After picking up a menu and finding that breakfast was available, I quickly placed an order and shopped around for some other things. While shopping, I noticed a cool T-shirt featuring a likeness of the famous bear for which the store was named. The owner, Leo Dunlavy, had stopped in and took an interest in my story. We talked about the usual things and then I asked about the famous bear. Leo filled me in on the "bear facts." The world's record black bear, dressing out at 665 pounds and standing 7 feet 10 inches tall, was killed near Glidden in 1963. Thus followed the bear being chosen as the town's mascot and its claim as the "Black Bear Capital of the Wisconsin." Leo gave me a T-shirt.

He also told me about his desire to snowmobile around Lake Superior one day, and I mentioned my own desire to bike around all the Great Lakes. I had such an enjoyable time with Leo, Amy and Shannon that this overnight stay ranks as one of the very best of the whole trip. Anybody who visits this area should stop in for an interesting time. There was no cell coverage in the area but the motel had excellent WiFi.

The next morning, I headed east on Wisconsin 13. This

was the last cold morning and as always when cold, I hoped for the sun to get above the horizon. It seemed to take forever this time. Just before leaving town, I wanted to get a good picture of the famous stuffed bear inside his glass case. I don't think it was the actual mascot bear but it was made to look the same size. Its case was lit and had lots of tricky angles, making it difficult for me to get a good picture. This had been my favorite town of the journey, once again deemed so because of the people.

I stopped early at a convenience store in Butternut, one that had lots of locals standing around talking near the front of the store. Only a wood stove was missing. The egg-and-cheese biscuit was the pre-made variety that started out with a slab of sausage in between. With no reason to linger, I hit the road as the morning air started to warm. Butternut was all about musky and walleye fishing, which would have been fun.

A much bigger town was Park Falls, and I found it interesting. The town sign on the western side declared Park Falls to be "the ruffled grouse capital of the world." Who knew? On the other end of town was a huge monument that had an interesting back story.

Affectionately called "Old Abe," a bald eagle had been caught and tamed before being presented to the 8th Wisconsin Infantry, Company C of the Union Army of the Civil War. The eagle was carried into more than 50 battles and skirmishes and survived despite being wounded three times. His statue, similar to the way he looked during battle right beside the American flag, was quite impressive. His monument also honors the prisoners of war and the missing in action from all wars.

The two smaller towns that followed were Filfield and Phillips, where I had a nice discussion about my ride and possible hazardous weather predicted again for that night. I didn't get the name of the man who told me about the weather prediction and should have because he caught my attention. More town signs that pointed away from the main road included Prentice, Ogema, Chelsea and Whittlesey. A huge billboard for Ogema was almost a joke, proclaiming it as "the gateway to the tallest hill in Wisconsin." I was not about to seek out that hill because the buttes had already provided enough challenges ending in just seeing more tall hills.

Shortly thereafter, I pulled over to use the bathroom at a "wayside," a low-budget rest stop that was common in Northwoods Wisconsin. Just as I was about to ride away, Steve Mayer walked up and asked about my ride. He gave his guidance from a cyclist's point of view for the rest of the trip including the best way to get into Green Bay, now just two days away. Steve also told me about the Ice Age Trail, a thousand-mile trail entirely within Wisconsin that highlighted leftover Ice Age traits. The trail passed through the area just behind the wayside. Steve said, "See, right over there is the trail!" I had not noticed it nor was there any signage to promote it. But there it was, clearly a good trail.

Most of the day included a moderate headwind, largely because I had headed south. A turn to the east was just ahead as the ride neared its end, a thought that included some sadness. I can see why some people just keep riding and don't have any real plans for returning home. I followed a blog written by a German cyclist who I had met on my cross country ride for most of a year. Then one day, he gave it up, sold the bike and flew home abruptly.

I rode into Medford, my stop for the night after 77 miles for the day. I had called ahead to the Medford Inn and had been told that it was the least expensive motel in town. Ready to get off the bike, I stopped in the office and talked with the owner, Gary Jensen. A talkative guy, he told me about his best cycling memory, not of himself but of a 79-year-old lady who showed up in Medford several years ago. She spent most of the winter at his motel while waiting to pursue her quest to visit the smallest town in all 50 states. Gary said she was nearly done but he never found out whether she completed her journey. Her vehicle for this quest was a bicycle.

A few readers over the last few days had asked me what I enjoyed most about the day other than the scenery and the people. I'll admit to spending a good part of the late afternoon envisioning a downhill entry into a town, plenty of food, submitting my pictures and stories and then walking about the area where I spend the night. But two of my biggest favorite activities are taking a stinging hot shower and answering all the messages from home. I like to check on the news from home and a little bit of national news and sports. The time off the bike is just as precious as the time on it.

I often spend some time planning for the next day just before heading for bed. Early in my cycling adventures, I worried about planning and staying on track quite a bit. Not so much anymore. I am often asked about the extent of my planning. Some folks are disappointed and surprised that I don't know weeks ahead where I will spend the night on any given day. Honestly, on many days, I don't where I will spend the night by early afternoon and just as you have read so far, it's sometimes much later than that. It is just part of the fun.

I made a few calls about a room for the next night, finding everything too expensive and some off my idea of the best route. One place wanted a $100 cash deposit, and another wouldn't let bikes in the room. Just for fun, I asked for explanations on these two practices. These cash deposits were implemented due to people trashing rooms, and the "no bikes" rule came from grease being left all over the carpet. I actually laughed at the guy about the grease on the carpet because there is no grease on a bike. Oiling the chain, which I would never do on carpet, is usually done with a lightweight clear oil and a rag. Either way, these places were in a town called Shawano. In a twist of fate, I didn't make it to Shawano anyway.

One call was to what appeared to be an out-of-the-way town called Tigerton. The price was good, and the motel looked fine in photos but it was way off the main road to Green Bay. That is just where I ended up, and here is how it happened.

On Thursday afternoon, Steve Mayer at the wayside advised me to do a couple of things when I left Medford. One was to take a couple of scenic country roads, and the other was to use Wisconsin 29 into Green Bay. I went to bed confident of his advice. A longtime Wisconsin friend had advised me to find another route because of the high traffic level on 29 in certain areas. Always willing to take a chance, I was not worried about the traffic. It would be another adventure, or so I thought. Turns out it was an adventure but of a much different sort.

Gary Jensen had told me that he took special pride in making breakfast for everyone at the motel. He owned the next-door dairy bar and made scones daily for anyone interested. I thought the idea was wonderful and loaded my bike before walking it over to the dairy bar. Gary was inside but still a long way from having anything prepared. Daylight was coming, and I needed to be going.

Just down the street was Kwik Trip, my favorite convenience store. This time, I found an amazing veggie omelet biscuit for $2.69. A few 33-cents-per-pound bananas and some other items completed my purchases. I realized that I had paid twice that banana price at the grocery store across the street the night before.

I did discover that Medford was the home of Jeane Dixon, famous astrologer and psychic. The town also has a curling club, probably something way more popular in the Northwoods.

I rode away, quite content with that giant biscuit, and planned to follow Steve's directions. He told me to get off Wisconsin 13 soon because of construction and take county roads A and C and connect with 29 that way. Those roads were my first venture by bike into Wisconsin dairy country. The Northwoods appeared to be behind me now, but I was not sure. Milking cows was in progress as I rode by the farms so early in the morning. I found Wisconsin 29 and pointed my bike toward Green Bay.

The early riding on 29 was fine with a good shoulder and steady traffic. A car pulled over ahead of me, and I realized it was Steve Mayer. He said, "I thought I would see you again this morning. Got everything you need?" I told him I did and thanked him for stopping. Steve and his daughter were headed into Green Bay to help set up a wedding.

Riding continued to be good for the next 20 miles and I began to think, much too soon, that this was going to be an easy day. Shortly afterwards, I saw the sign that I had dreaded. Wisconsin 29 was set to become a freeway with "No pedestrians and non-motorized vehicles allowed." While this was bad news, I thought of Jack Day back in

Montana on his bicycle. I guess if he passed this way, Jack could keep right on riding since he had a motor. The highway was about to pass through Wausau, so I had only two choices. I could claim that I didn't see the sign and, if not stopped, I would make fast progress. Or, as I decided to do, I could pull off at Marathon City and follow a slower route through the countryside. That route looked more direct as the crow flies but I knew it would have rolling hills and multiple road changes.

My decision to take the backroad route certainly didn't come from an aversion to heavy traffic, having seen plenty on other rides and as recently as Fargo on this one. The dicey part was crossing through traffic for on and off ramps, hoping that my signals to traffic were being seen. Plus, I had been stopped at least twice before by law enforcement on this type of road, and I didn't want to relive the last one in Illinois. That highway patrolman held me up for quite a while doing whatever kind of checking he could do on me from my driver's license.

Thinking that I had a fast start on the day, I chose to take a few minutes to eat again at McDonald's. Mapping out my route would be a next best thing to do and I thought it was worth the time. After getting my food, I started to eat and study the maps. A little boy was with his grandmother and as they headed for a table, he dropped his ice water. He just kept going and sat down, just as did his grandmother. The ice and water covered a good section of the floor. No one seemed to pay any attention so I got up and grabbed some napkins and started to wipe up the water and ice. The boy saw me and went over and got some napkins, too and started to help. He really seemed to enjoy the work and soon had the floor polished. In the meantime, I had sat back down. His grandmother mouthed a "Thank you" as I finished my food and started to head out.

I grabbed my iPad from the bike and went back to talk with them. Beth Sommer and grandson Otto were from Edgar, the next town over. I told them that I would write about them for a North Carolina paper and had a pleasant conversation. Once they had my card, I knew they would check the website the next day. That was another pleasant encounter during a day that would have a few twists.

The new route looked doable as I rode into Marathon City. I wondered about the town's name and read that the Battle of Marathon that founded the legend of Phidippides was the inspiration. Just to confirm my plan, I saw a police officer coming out of a store in town and pulled over to ask him about the route. Officer Chris Koeppl assured me that I needed to avoid 29 and especially that part through Wausau that my friend had mentioned. He told me that the road ahead was good and included some hills. Even though I had seen the huge hill climbing out of town, I couldn't really appreciate just how big it was because nothing else around was like it. But, just for giggles as my nephew would say, my road went right straight up that hill. Officer Koeppl laughed and said, "Yep, right up there, just over the top is your next turn." I knew he would be watching me climb it. I hope he did because right up that hill I went, breathing hard but not about to stop and rest.

More similar hills followed for a while until I rode past the Granite Peak Ski Area. Very soon things started to calm down as I pedaled into Mosinee, big enough for an interstate highway and an airport. I turned onto Wisconsin 153 and almost had the road to myself, except for a garbage truck that used one of those automated arms to pick up trash bins. He kept leapfrogging me. There were enough houses to keep him darting in front of me and I had to swing out and go around him. It was not a big deal though because few other vehicles seemed to use this road. It was like Montana traffic, and I was making good time again.

Just as earlier in the day, all that quickly changed. I pedaled toward a "Road Closed Ahead" sign, not too worried initially but wondering if the lack of traffic had something to do with this. With my reasonable past success of riding though the detours and Road Closed signs, I just kept pedaling. As I neared the very small town of Bevent, I saw that this road was really closed and that a truck with flashing lights was guarding it ahead. I saw a pickup truck about to enter the road from a driveway and stopped to ask the driver and passenger what had happened and would I be able to get though. The two men told me not to try it, that the road was flooded and had been for a few days. I needed to do a work-around that would bring me back to 153 on the other side of town. I followed directions for once and after a mile, saw a woman getting mail from her box and stopped to ask her if I was on the right track. She seemed to enjoy our conversation and told me what had happened. It seems a farmer had tried to dam up a creek and it had worked for a while, but eventually the dam broke and water rushed through the area enough to flood the road. She assured me that no one was happy because the real detour was quite long. But for me to just get to the other side of town, all I had to do was take a couple of left turns and eventually I would come out on 153 past the flooded area. After about four miles out of the way, I rejoined the road and continued east. Part of the four miles was on a loose gravel road that caused some uncertain riding. My loaded bike does not like gravel.

The next town was Elderon, which had less than 200 residents, same as most other towns in the area. I didn't see a store but really didn't need one except for water. I did find a nice ballfield with a community center and hoped to find water there. I didn't, but after a bathroom stop, I just kept pedaling. The last part of 153 ran through some of the prettiest country that I had seen recently but the road seemed forgotten by any maintenance program. The pavement was really bad with huge breaks and bumps as I pedaled past an excessively rocky area. That finally ended as I found an easterly turn on Wisconsin 45.

Remember the motel that seemed to be my best choice the night before? The out of the way one in Tigerton? That is exactly where I spent the night after 94 miles on an unusual day. If I had pursued one of those strange on-the-planned-route hotels in Shawano, I would have still had miles to go. I found the owner of the Rock a Bye Inn to be a great guy. He put me in a spacious room that was very suitable for my last night on the road before the pedaling ended. The motel was a mile away from the town of Tigerton. The owner told me how to find the grocery store and convenience store. Just about out of supplies and with no remaining water, I rode toward town. Tigerton is named for Tiger Creek that has fast-running waters that supposedly roar like a tiger.

Interesting things were not yet over for the day. I found the Cedar Street Market, the grocery store, first and looked for some healthy choices. The grocery was small but it had some good things, both in food and people. Before I left, I had talked to everyone in the store, and clerk Kerrie made sure I had some good stuff in my bags. I left there still needing ice because the motel didn't have any. I rode across town and stopped at the convenience store to get some. The motel owner had advised me to go to the grocery store instead of the convenience store and I might have found out why. I looked around and didn't see any ice dispenser, odd in an area that can sometimes get pretty hot. It was certainly hot on this day. I asked the clerk for ice and told her that I was on a bike and just needed a couple of large cups filled to the brim. She seemed to think that was odd and offered to show me where the big bags of ice were. I thought that was odd. No need for a bag of ice on a bike.

There was a restaurant next door and I went there and asked for a Diet Coke and a couple of cups of ice. There was an elderly waitress working, and she took such an interest in my order that she filled it right away and came back with everything, saying "That will be $1." I loved her attitude and gave her a $5 bill and told her that the rest was for her. Her smile was worth much more as she continued to thank me. I had my ice and headed back to the motel room, now about a mile and a half away.

My last night on the road was about to begin. The room was so comfortable and roomy that I set up my food and worked on the day's update. I kept reflecting on the many highlights and challenges of the journey, just as I often do as the last few miles draw near. On my Underground Railroad adventure, I had only 20 miles to ride on the last day and kept delaying the final moments when it would be time to step off the bike. Once this next-to-last-day's update was complete, I answered some messages and took my shower before heading to bed. It had been one of my favorite days even if nothing turned out as planned. If one single day ever needed to be used as a significant example of "a seat of the pants day," this was it. As usual, I slept well. One riding day remained.

As the days had dwindled on the trip, Allison Tuck from

Travels by Allison in Lexington, N.C., had been exploring the best way for me to get home from Green Bay. One-way flights and even round-trip flights out of the Green Bay airport to Charlotte or Greensboro were extremely high priced. As always, when I finished a ride in some state far away, it was not only an issue of getting me home but also the bike. Allison began to explore renting a car for the one-way trip a few days before. She was able to find a real deal on a car but the timing was off. Allison went to work on getting the same rate moved to my target date for leaving Wisconsin. With her knowledge and a little luck, we had a car arranged at the airport for first thing Sunday morning. I planned to arrive in Green Bay on this Friday afternoon, spend some time sightseeing on Saturday, get a good rest that night and drive nearly 1,000 miles on Sunday. No need to ship the bike because it was going to ride along with me.

My last day of pedaling began with more miles on Wisconsin 45. As soon as I rode back through Tigerton, I realized that the road was being paved ahead. It started out as a few miles of roughed-up pavement leading to new asphalt that had been applied for about seven more miles. I expect that I was the first bike to ride on this new pavement, and it was a wonderful gift on this special day. Brand new pavement makes the bike ride like a good car, smooth and quiet.

The first town I encountered was Marion, still on a very good road. I spotted a huge chicken that looked to be tied down by ropes. All of this was right beside the road next to a large convenience store. With such a huge chicken, I figured there had to be great breakfast sandwiches here. After a celebratory breakfast of egg sandwiches and Amish pastries, I was ready for some serious riding.

On into Clintonville on 45 gave way to a left turn on S.R. 22 and Main Street. Another "Detour Ahead" sign made me think that this one would be a piece of cake to get around. How could town officials totally block a road that had sidewalks and houses on both sides? First off, I discovered that the pavement was gone and that I was riding on smooth dirt, then rough dirt followed by big holes in the road that forced me onto the sidewalk. Eventually even the sidewalk was gone. I pushed my bike through a couple of yards until machinery and piles of dirt even blocked that. With a walk through a side yard, I was able to access S.R. 156. I got a few mean stares along the "Road Closed" journey, but again I made it through. The reason for all the work appeared to be replacing or repairing the town water line. I wondered if all those houses on the street even had water.

On 156, I found a nearly deserted road except for plenty of horseflies. They began to circle the bike, and I couldn't ride fast enough to get away. While they stayed close, only a few landed on me and tried to bite. Briarton had little activity and almost no stores, but Navarino had an impressive baseball field. There were no bathrooms or water available though. I also passed plenty of beautiful old barns and working farms along the way.

By following 156, I was able to intersect again with Wisconsin 29, the bigger and faster road that I had to leave just before Wausau the previous morning. At this point, 29 had plenty of non-freeway characteristics but it also had plenty of traffic. Drivers could make U-turns and drive completely across 29 from side-roads. No signs prohibited bikes.

My pace into Green Bay was pretty fast, largely because of there being no reason to stop and a good shoulder. The last 15 miles flew by. I had only to enter Green Bay, find my way through a maze of roads and then just two more streets to pass through the heart of downtown before pedaling out to Bay Beach Amusement Park. The park would be the site of my ceremonial front wheel dipping marking the end of my trip.

But first things first, with less than four miles left in the journey, I thought that the bumpy road had everything to do with the pavement. When my pedaling didn't produce the speed that it should, I realized that my back tire was going flat. Having practiced the rear tire tube change just a few days earlier in Minnesota, I found a front yard in which to lay the bike over and started the process. I called my friends who were waiting at the amusement park and told them that I would be there a half-hour late. It was amazing how much easier taking the tire off and swapping the tube was when horseflies and mosquitos weren't around. This was by far the quickest tire repair I had ever done. This flat was the third of the ride, continuing my long-time average of about one per 1,000 miles. Once the repair was completed and the ride nearly done, I had one extra replacement tube and one CO2 cartridge. Close enough for me.

Back on the bike, I rode on toward my final destination. These roads were familiar because I had spent plenty of time in Green Bay. I had no trouble riding through the streets except for some spots of bad pavement. The sight of the amusement park ahead didn't bring a tear as the final destination has before. I looked closer and spotted my host family beside the road, both of them clapping and cheering me on.

I'll share more details in the next chapter, but Kathy and Dave Mikulsky are great friends and they had both been a tremendous help in planning the last part of this ride. I stopped at the edge of the park, and we all hugged each other. I walked the bike on into the amusement park with the Mikulskys at my side. They had already picked the best place to dip the front tire, and we headed there to get the formalities out of the way.

The huge Smith family was enjoying the park that day, and the dad, Jeff, was especially interested in my bike ride. All seven family members stayed with us until I rolled the tire into the water, and plenty of pictures were made. The family included Jeff, his wife, Amanda, their kids, Rosalie, Graham, Eloise and Curtis and Jeff's mom, Leah Williams.

The wheel had been dipped and the 2017 ride across northwestern America was complete.

CHAPTER 11

Sightseeing in Wisconsin, by car this time, and the long drive home

With the official duties of my ride now complete, it was very easy to relax. Dave Mikulsky and I worked for the same company out of Green Bay for about 11 years. He lived in Green Bay, site of the national office, and I lived in Rowan County and managed the plant there. Dave headed up purchasing and we had plenty of opportunities to talk about business matters. But more than that, we had become friends during the very early days of my employment. As a requirement of the job, I had to attend training from January through March in Green Bay and work at the facilities there.

I was a southern boy, born and bred, and had never experienced anything like a Green Bay winter. I was hired in December and was expected to spend the next 12 weeks in a cold area, but I realistically had no idea what that cold would be like. I had flown to Green Bay twice before, and both times the weather was not much colder than we occasionally see in North Carolina. Honestly, I was shocked to step off that plane in early January and feel the wind and single-digit temperatures. I was a serious runner, planning to run at least once a day, every day. My idea of running clothing for cold weather was just an extra layer or two of the things that I wore while running at home. Very quickly, I realized that I needed more than that. So did Dave. As a runner himself, he brought me some things that would help. Kathy and Dave came to my motel room, and I knew immediately that I liked them and was especially glad to have two new friends a thousand miles from home.

We both ended up leaving the company, 11 years later for me and a few more than that for Dave. We stayed in touch, however, and when I had an opportunity to visit the area for another venture last year, the three of us picked up right where we had left off. As plans came together for my current bike journey, I was drawn toward an ending in Wisconsin. And if that was the case, why not do it in Green Bay? The idea grew and finally fell into part of the plan. I would pedal to Green Bay, where Kathy and Dave had agreed to help me with a night or two of lodging and with getting back home.

On Friday, July 21, 40 days after I had pedaled east from Anacortes, Washington, we loaded my bike in Dave's car. My riding had ended but I had also been looking forward to my plans with Kathy and Dave. We had planned a big day of sightseeing for Saturday. Even though I had been to the Green Bay area many times, I had still not seen all the sights, so Dave and Kathy had a busy schedule for us.

We headed back to their house, and while I took a shower, Kathy washed my clothes. One shirt and at least one pair of socks probably should have just been thrown away but she made them all look nice. We went out to dinner and then back to their house, where we talked for hours once my update for that day was sent in to the Salisbury Post. I still planned an update on the bonus day of sightseeing by car. My time in the Green Bay area had been nearly all about work. I had never ventured north of the city for any distance. We were going to do that on Saturday.

An interesting twist on the day included two folks from home. Dick Franklin had been a friend of mine for years, and he kept up with my riding while traveling extensively on his own in an RV. We had just missed each other a couple of times on previous trips. This time, he was in the Green Bay area for the Oshkosh Air Adventure Fly-In with his sister, Wanda. Dick had told us that we could meet on Saturday, and Dave offered to drive us all around for most of the day.

After a stop at Kwik Trip, also a favorite of the Mikulskys, we headed to Lambeau Field, home of the Green Bay Packers. We didn't know that a road race was going on that morning at the stadium and found the parking lot jammed with cars. Just as we pulled into the huge lot, I got a text from Dick and quickly realized that he had parked just a few feet away from us. Introductions were made all the way around, and we all loaded into Dave's car for the ride north.

I told everyone how I knew Dave and Kathy and how I had gotten to know Dick. We also found out a little about Wanda as we rode north. She was in training to be a pilot, something with which Dick was helping. She was actually using his plane for the flight time. Both were going to attend the E.A.A. Air Adventure Fly-In, an annual event for Dick who is a member of the Experimental Aircraft Association.

We all rode in the Mikulsky chariot north toward Door County, a place that I had heard of for years but never visited. The county is bordered on both sides by water and made up of small touristy towns. We rode through Egg Harbor, Fish Creek and into Sister Bay on the way to Al Johnson's Swedish Restaurant, which Dick had recommended. Two things made the restaurant special. Goats grazed on the roof of the restaurant that specialized in Swedish pancakes and meatball dishes. We waited an hour for a table but made good use of that time by walking around the harbor. Of course, I had the pancakes.

Door County is also quite famous for its specialized produce. Cherries were being freshly harvested, and we stopped for cherry pies and jams at Seaquist Orchards Farm Market. The cherry pies were quite heavy. Dick bought us slices of cherry pie that were so full of cherries that they could have been used for a good wrist curl workout. This area in Door County reminded me of the New England coast, with its cool towns and water views.

After another stop for our choices of ice cream or custard, we dropped off Dick and Wanda so that they could head back to Oshkosh and their RV. The fly-in didn't officially start for two more days but the crowd was already building and setup was well under way. Dave, Kathy and I decided to ride over there, too, and see if we could get in and walk among the pre-event activities. We all hoped to see some of the historic planes that had already arrived.

Dave is a U.S. Army Vietnam War veteran who recently received an honor flight to Washington. He wore his commemorative shirt and cap, and we got quick access to walk around the grounds. Over the next three hours, we walked 10,000 steps and watched planes landing two to three at a time in advance of the opening, now just a day and a half away. Warbird planes were the big draw and several were already in place.

Our big highlights were seeing and meeting the crews of an Army Chinook helicopter and an Air Force B-52 bomber. Dave had witnessed the work of earlier models of both aircraft in Vietnam. Most interesting was our talk with Army Chief Warrant Officer 2 Forrest Woodbury.

Visiting the Adventure Fly-In grounds whet my appetite for more. Through another venture of my own, chronicled in the book "Young Again," I spent much of 2016 flying around the country in a historic WWII-era Stearman biplane. This experience has endeared me even more to the world of flight. Soon, I will attend the fly-in when it is officially open.

Back to the Mikulsky home, we had a quiet evening filled with a lot more talking. It had been years since we had spent this much time together, but as with most major-league friendships, time passed much too quickly and soon it was time for bed. In anticipation of my longest driving challenge ever, we turned in and gratefully reflected on our very pleasant time together. My meager bags were packed, and I was ready to head home now after 42 days away.

Allison Tuck had worked her magic, getting a great rate on the one-way SUV back to North Carolina on the day that I needed it. Not totally sure that things would work out, I prayed that evening that they would. I was excited about driving almost 1,000 miles in one day, all alone.

The next day, I got up early and with a few nice snacks and drinks supplied by Kathy and Dave, I loaded the bike in Dave's car. After a hug from Kathy, I got in the car and we headed for the Green Bay airport. The airport was not busy this early on a Sunday morning. Dave waited while I went to get my car at the rental desk. At exactly 8 a.m., the rental clerk came in for work. I got my car for the right price with the only surprise being a super high airport tax. The lady behind me in line said that Green Bay's airport actually had one of the lowest tax rates around the country.

Back in the lot, Dave and I loaded the bike and my other stuff, including food and drinks. After another hug and handshake, I hit the road. Dave had helped me with what he thought was the best route and my research matched well. On the road finally, I was excited to be headed home.

Just as with my bicycle trip, I was ready to do this long drive, something that I had struggled with in earlier times. I once fell asleep on a long drive and slept through a car crash into the woods. I was just one exit from home when it happened. Another time, with my daughters in the car, I fell asleep and nearly hit a big truck on the interstate. Most importantly, I knew that there was no time to waste as I hoped to make it home to unload the car and return it to the Charlotte airport within 24 hours. As you can imagine, my regular prayer that began each morning of cycling was a part of the car drive, too. "Lord, ride with me today! Keep me safe and help me to make it today."

I rode through Milwaukee, Chicago and Indianapolis. Then a time zone change, a few storms, Columbus, Ohio, and Charleston, West Virginia. I reflected, ate and stopped briefly a few times for a bathroom and a Diet Coke with caffeine. I rolled into my own driveway at 11:30 p.m. that night after only one traffic slowdown along the way. I unloaded the bike and my gear. It felt great to be home!

After five hours of sleep, I woke up quickly and returned the car to the Charlotte airport. I had driven a total of 995 miles! I had not anticipated sleeping at home and expected to pull off the side of the road a few times before barely making it to Charlotte in time. But as with all my prayers, God was with me. I never once even yawned, something that I had expected to happen often once it got dark. Amazing! Much of the time, I listened to talk radio, sports and gospel music. All of it worked. My daughter, Amber, was there to bring me home. I spent the day going through newspapers, mail, home phone messages and anything else that needed doing. I reintroduced myself to the horses.

Another cycling adventure was truly complete!

A less-than-perfect selfie as Freeze tried to hold up the bike and take a photo to start the ride in Anacortes, Washington. As with much of this ride, no one else was around.

It was cold on top of Washington Pass at 5,477 feet.

Police Chief Paul Budrow in Twisp, Washington, was a big help with directions with a road closed situation ahead.

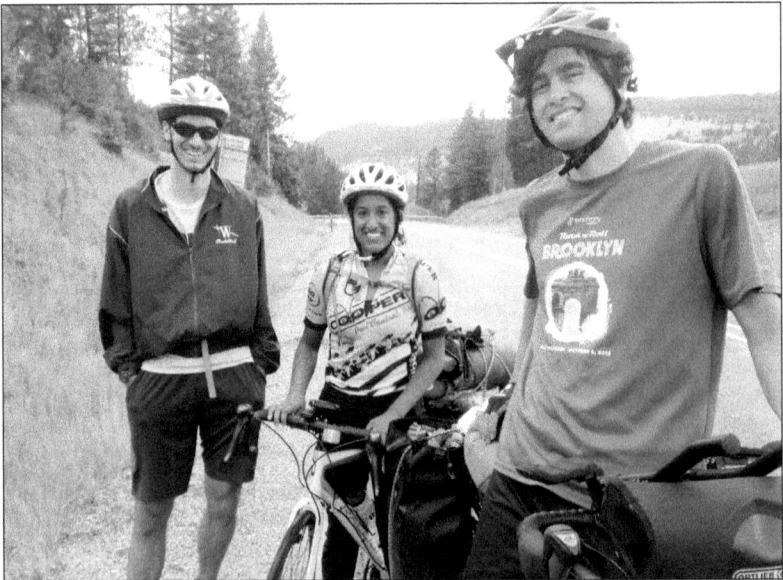

From left: Joe Podurgiel, Sonali Rodriguez and Brett Lehner were on the road as Freeze pedaled over the Wauconda Pass and into Republic, Washington.

216

This old church in Hope, Idaho, was now used almost exclusively as a wedding chapel. There was no need to hang around.

This was the favorite stop for food on the whole trip with Beth Morkert at the Big Sky Pantry.

217

The Libby Dam on the Kootenai River near Libby, Montana.

Jack Day, age 74, was on the way to San Francisco on his motorized bicycle.

218

One of the endless beautiful scenes in Glacier National Park.

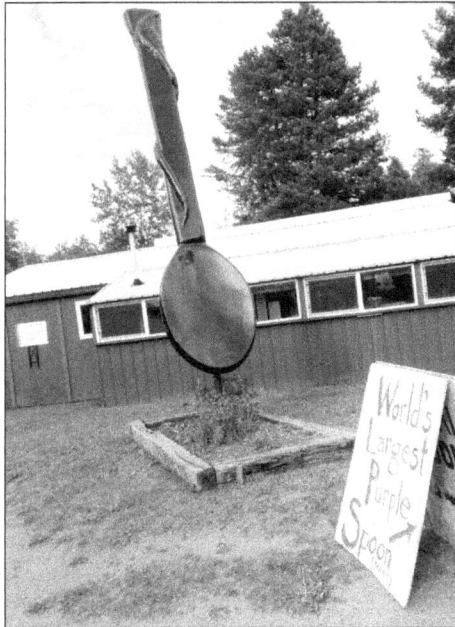

The World's Largest Purple Spoon in East Glacier, Montana.

A sunrise in Big Sky country

Tarryn Wickens, left, from London and Bastien Tren Hoste from Belgium were following the Northern Tier route.

Teddy Roosevelt's restored cabin called the Maltese Cross sits beside the visitor center in the Teddy Roosevelt National Park, Medora, N.D.

Best sign seen on the whole journey was in Newell, S.D.

221

An early morning view of Mt. Rushmore near Rapid City, S.D.

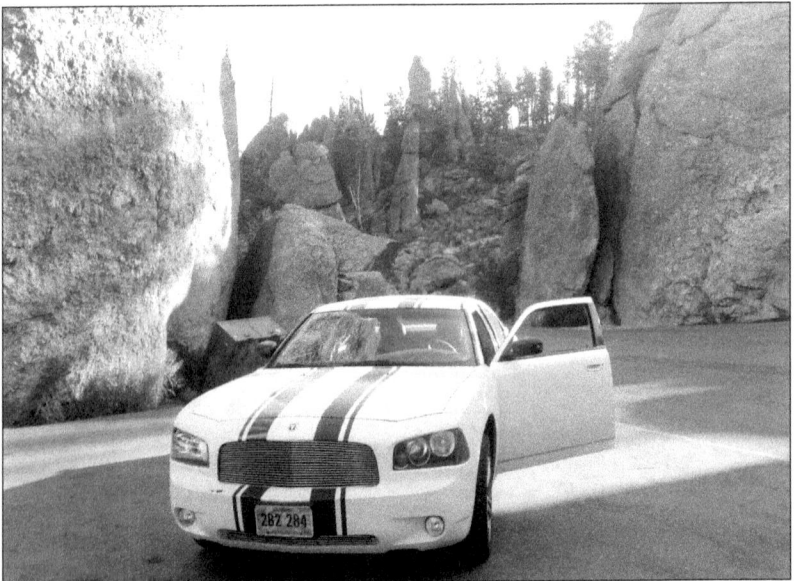

A borrowed car made it possible to see all the Rapid City, S.D., tourist sites in one day.

Rock formations in Custer State Park, S.D.

The Crazy Horse Memorial, also near Rapid City, S.D.

223

Downtown Deadwood, S.D., where Wild Bill Hickok and Calamity Jane roamed the streets.

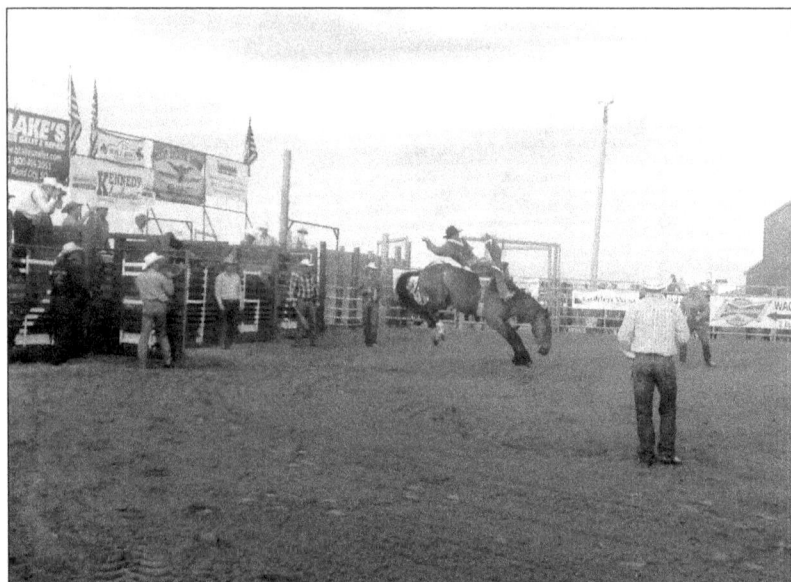

Freeze's first-ever Fourth of July rodeo while on a cycling trip was in Interior, S.D., in the heart of the Badlands.

The Twin Bing, King Bing and Patriotic Bing candy bars were a highlight from the trip and are now sold back in Salisbury.

The Mississippi River headwaters at Lake Itasca, Minnesota.

Remer, Minnesota, home of Bigfoot.

Boardwalk and bike path in Duluth, Minnesota, with Lake Superior in the background.

Bill Huckabee of Sweetwater, Texas, was riding to Canada and back.

The Roger Maris Museum in Fargo was a favorite stop. Maris eclipsed Babe Ruth's single season home run record.

From left: Leo Dunlavy, Shannon Mertig and Amy Crom all work at the Bear Crossing Convenience Store in Glidden, Wisconsin, a favorite town and store.

The statue in Park Falls, Wisconsin, of Old Abe commemorates a tamed bald eagle that was carried into battle by the 8th Wisconsin Infantry during the Civil War. Old Abe saw action in over 50 battles and was wounded three times.

Steve Mayer from Medford, Wisconsin, gave great directions one afternoon and then stopped to check on Freeze the next day on the way to Green Bay.

This giant chicken attracted drivers who needed a big breakfast near Marion, Wisconsin.

The Bay Beach Amusement Park was the end of the line and the location of the ceremonial front wheel dipping in Green Bay, Wisconsin.

The Smith family helped celebrate the end of the cycling adventure in Green Bay.

From left: Kathy Mikulsky, Wanda Huntley, Dick Franklin and Dave Mikulsky on a day of sightseeing in Door County, Wisconsin. Huntley and Franklin are from Salisbury, N.C., and the Mikulsky family are Freeze's long-time friends.

Freeze and the flight crew of a B-52 bomber at the EAA Airventure Oshkosh 2017 fly-in.

233

EPILOGUE

Back home again, safe and sound

I had already pegged the Northwest Territory as the venue for my 2017 cycling adventure. It was the first time that I had known the ride location for more than a year in advance. This was the logical next step to add more states to my cycling resumé but it was much more than that. Only in two of the states, Idaho and Montana, had I spent any time cycling before. The rest of the states were all new, including Washington, North and South Dakota, Nebraska, Iowa, Minnesota and Wisconsin. As much as I think I know about new areas, I always discover way more in terms of wonderful people, scenery and an overall awareness of grassroots America.

People — it always comes back to the people. I have said time and again, my early misconception of cycling through new areas would bring a great reward of vistas of scenery that I could only have dreamed of before. Certainly this does happen, but it is the people, the real Americans that I continue to meet along the way. I hesitate to mention a few of them because others may be left out. Still, I can't move on without mentioning some of the folks I encountered along my northwest adventure.

Andy Heckathorn, a cyclist in the Fargo area, pulled over to wait for me as he was driving through the morning rush hour. His willingness to provide information helped me to move on from the cloud of uncertainty of that morning as I headed into yet another remote area. I had several choices, none of which seemed right until I was able to talk with Andy. He convinced me to make the right calls and off I went through at least two successful days because of his influence.

Bill Goodgion, of Rapid City, helped me with several dilemmas as I approached and visited western South Dakota. His offer of assistance for a mechanical issue and a desire to see much more in a day than I could have on a bike, plus advice on a place to stay and sightseeing details, were exceptional. I used his car for that special day and met all my goals.

A motel owner, Chris Zaferes, not only offered me a great room and plenty of interesting conversation, he called ahead to check on possible accommodations for the next night. I loved hearing the reflections he offered on living in New York City and running the New York City Marathon.

Among the pleasant surprises was Beth Morkert and her Big Sky Pantry. I regret to this day that I did not buy several times the amount of wonderful baked goods from her out-of-the-way location. She brightened my day immeasurably with her smile and conversation.

From the poor selfie that documented the beginning of my official tide to well-planned rear tire dipping in Green Bay, I had a wonderful time. Imagine all those things that happen on a bike: three flat tires, the bugs, flies and mosquitoes, the thundering abuse of dead-on headwinds, heavy rains, lightning, and for the first time ever, hail — all are things that you can usually avoid in a car. Add to that the many "Road Closed" signs and the adventures that sometimes happen when getting around them. But somehow, I got through every single one even though the odds were against me. The gravel shoulders and poor roads wouldn't have mattered much in a car but certainly changed my approach on the bike.

I found enough bike shops to get the supplies I needed although it was touch and go a few times. The bike itself, other than a relatively minor shifting issue, did exactly what I expected of it once again. I totally endorse a Surly Long Haul Trucker to anyone considering doing this type of endurance ride. The issue of the mechanical problem with the cyclometer forced me to fall back to counting mile markers and Google distances. To fix it, I had to learn how to take it apart and manipulate the small parts, another good thing. The rest of my list of specialized equipment did the expected job once again. Not one thing would I change as the thought of my next ride begins.

The results of any riding issues I encountered was the ability to see America again at an average pace of 10-12 mph. Just a few of the incredible visuals were Mt. Rushmore, the Crazy Horse Memorial, Glacier National Park with its amazing snowy panoramas, more of the Montana "Big Sky" vastness, the Badlands and the Washington and Sherman passes. I saw the Roger Maris museum, more national parks and rode on parts of the coast-to-coast U.S. 2. I plan to ride more of it one day.

Physical challenges were many, but never overwhelming. The almost daily uphill riding — once as much as nearly 5,000 feet in a day — and the remoteness of most of the ride and occasional struggles to get supplies and especially water as needed all mattered. Different from any of my other past rides was the wind. I somehow was naïve enough to expect that most of the wind would come from the west, just as it had in the past. And for the first time ever, I was actually concerned about my ability to make it through at least one major storm.

Two parts of each adventure on which I usually have the most fun are the motel and food searches. I have basic information about upcoming towns and some listing of motels as I ride, but being so budget challenged makes me search for the best deal available. Sometimes, I just had to ask for it. As you read in the book, I found some great places and enjoyed tremendously almost every night of planning and rest.

Food, on the other hand, was always subject to availability, space and weight. Only on a few occasions did I run low enough on either water or food to get concerned. The license to eat such a large volume of food, including lesser healthy choices is fun and a little bit comedic. Never too far from being hungry, the ongoing search for more calories takes precedent over most other issues. F'real milkshakes and Twin Bings were my favorite new foods discovered on the trip. Dairy Queen pineapple milkshakes are still my favorite treat.

There are numerous towns that I plan to visit again but a few stood out as my favorites. Republic, Washington, was perfect on a chilly, rainy afternoon during my first week of riding. Interior, South Dakota, in the Badlands offered my long-awaited Fourth of July rodeo and the warmest day on the ride. Glidden, Wisconsin, made the cut because I saw my first live bear, met some great people and loved the overnight experience of the town.

Little things mattered as they always do. The traffic was never really an issue and drivers were without a doubt the most considerate of all my riding adventures to date. Long periods without seeing a vehicle on the road became quite nice once I got used to it. Good shoulders, the always appreciated but seldom experienced tailwind, and general good weather helped make this ride one of the best. I found the state signs I needed amid bigger challenges than I expected.

Ending in Wisconsin and spending time with friends

Dave and Kathy Mikulsky was the perfect ending for yet another cycling adventure. The sightseeing and general wind-down from the challenge of the road came to an end just as it should with a certain calmness and sense of achievement.

As of this writing, two months after the end of my ride, I have no lingering health issues following plenty of good rest and better nutrition once off the road. Health issues had been quite serious at the end of several previous journeys. I suspect that it won't be long before yet another adventure comes together. In fact, a few are already in mind although I don't yet know where the next long ride will go. Alaska, Hawaii, Vermont, Nevada and Utah remain at the top of my list so they will soon be in the mix.

When it comes time, I look forward to riding again with the confidence and peace of God as I embark on yet another journey. And without a doubt, I hope you will ride along with me again!

"Have I not commanded you? Be strong and courageous. Do not be frightened and do not be dismayed, for the Lord your God is with you wherever you go."

—Joshua 1:9

THANK THE LORD!

A prayer by Scott Weant — 7/21/17

Thank the Lord for riding with David again, each and every day.

Thank the Lord for providing a place every night to get the rest needed for the next day's ride.

Thank the Lord for meeting his nutrition and hydration needs.

Thank the Lord for helping David make the bike repairs along the way.

Thank the Lord for giving him the strength, endurance, stamina and willpower to make each day's destination.

Thank the Lord for all the people David met during this year's ride.

Thank the Lord for helping him plan each day's ride.

Thank the Lord for all the beauty He provided along the way.

Thank the Lord for stories David was able to share so we could ride along.

Thank the Lord for memories from this year's ride and may they last a lifetime.

Thank the Lord for David's sponsors.

Thank the Lord for getting him home safe and sound.

ABOUT THE AUTHOR

It was time to go riding again and cycling across the northwest was the perfect fit. More than anything, another adventure awaited with six more as yet uncycled states in the crosshairs. This is the author's sixth book, all chronicling travel and adventure of some sort, as well as his compelling interaction with backroads Americans along the way. David Freeze has not been everywhere yet but he's adding to his list. When all 50 states across America are done, what and where will be the next adventure? You can bet he's working on it now.

David is also a motivational speaker, emphasizing that regular people can achieve amazing things. Contact him at david.freeze@ctc.net. Walnut Creek Farm Publishing is named after his farm.

An accomplished runner and endurance cyclist, David has written four other books that cover various adventures across America by bicycle. He has completed over 82,000 running miles and 15,000 endurance cycling miles.

Other books by David Freeze include:

- **Lord, Ride with Me Today**
  The story of a solo coast-to-coast bicycle journey — 2013

- **Pedaling, Prayers and Perseverance**
  35 Days Cycling Solo from Maine to Key West — 2014

- **Riding the Rails to Freedom**
  Cycling the Underground Railroad Route from Alabama to Ontario — 2015

- **Highway to History**
  A Cycling Adventure on Route 66 — 2016

- **Young Again**
  Veterans recapture a moment of youth through
  Ageless Aviation Dreams Foundation — 2017

www.ingramcontent.com/pod-product-compliance
Lightning Source LLC
LaVergne TN
LVHW051624080426
835511LV00016B/2164